CAMBRIDGE LIBRARY COLLECTION

Books of enduring scholarly value

Egyptology

The large-scale scientific investigation of Egyptian antiquities by Western scholars began as an unintended consequence of Napoleon's invasion of Egypt during which, in 1799, the Rosetta Stone was discovered. The military expedition was accompanied by French scholars, whose reports prompted a wave of enthusiasm that swept across Europe and North America resulting in the Egyptian Revival style in art and architecture. Increasing numbers of tourists visited Egypt, eager to see the marvels being revealed by archaeological excavation. Writers and booksellers responded to this growing interest with publications ranging from technical site reports to tourist guidebooks and from children's histories to theories identifying the pyramids as repositories of esoteric knowledge. This series reissues a wide selection of such books. They reveal the gradual change from the 'tomb-robbing' approach of early excavators to the highly organised and systematic approach of Flinders Petrie, the 'father of Egyptology', and include early accounts of the decipherment of the hieroglyphic script.

Inductive Metrology

Among the leading Egyptologists of his day, Sir William Matthew Flinders Petrie (1853–1942) excavated over fifty sites and trained a generation of archaeologists. As a young man, he demonstrated an aptitude for mathematics and used this skill to measure monuments across the south of England, including Stonehenge. Published in 1877, this work was based in part on these early surveys and provides great insight into the linear measurements used by ancient civilisations. Notably, Petrie establishes that accurate measurement was possible in societies without writing systems. His innovative approach to metrology draws comparisons between units of measurement used by peoples separated by great spans of time and distance, ranging from medieval Ireland to ancient Egypt. Petrie went on to write prolifically throughout his long career, and a great many of his other publications are also reissued in this series.

T0364271

Cambridge University Press has long been a pioneer in the reissuing of out-of-print titles from its own backlist, producing digital reprints of books that are still sought after by scholars and students but could not be reprinted economically using traditional technology. The Cambridge Library Collection extends this activity to a wider range of books which are still of importance to researchers and professionals, either for the source material they contain, or as landmarks in the history of their academic discipline.

Drawing from the world-renowned collections in the Cambridge University Library and other partner libraries, and guided by the advice of experts in each subject area, Cambridge University Press is using state-of-the-art scanning machines in its own Printing House to capture the content of each book selected for inclusion. The files are processed to give a consistently clear, crisp image, and the books finished to the high quality standard for which the Press is recognised around the world. The latest print-on-demand technology ensures that the books will remain available indefinitely, and that orders for single or multiple copies can quickly be supplied.

The Cambridge Library Collection brings back to life books of enduring scholarly value (including out-of-copyright works originally issued by other publishers) across a wide range of disciplines in the humanities and social sciences and in science and technology.

Inductive Metrology

*Or, The Recovery of Ancient Measures
from the Monuments*

W.M. Flinders Petrie

CAMBRIDGE
UNIVERSITY PRESS

CAMBRIDGE
UNIVERSITY PRESS

University Printing House, Cambridge, CB2 8BS, United Kingdom

Published in the United States of America by Cambridge University Press, New York

Cambridge University Press is part of the University of Cambridge.
It furthers the University's mission by disseminating knowledge in the pursuit of
education, learning and research at the highest international levels of excellence.

www.cambridge.org
Information on this title: www.cambridge.org/9781108065764

© in this compilation Cambridge University Press 2013

This edition first published 1877
This digitally printed version 2013

ISBN 978-1-108-06576-4 Paperback

INDUCTIVE METROLOGY.

INDUCTIVE METROLOGY;

OR,

THE RECOVERY OF ANCIENT MEASURES FROM THE MONUMENTS.

BY

W. M. FLINDERS PETRIE.

LONDON:

HARGROVE SAUNDERS,

24, TICHBORNE STREET, REGENT QUADRANT.

1877.

PREFACE.

THIS essay has resulted from an attempt to determine the ancient standards of measure from the monuments: at first supposing that such a course would merely supply details; but afterwards finding that all, or nearly all, the recognised data of metrology could be thus independently ascertained; besides recovering a large amount of additional information.

No allusions have been made to volumes and weights, but only to linear quantities, as they alone are shown by the architectural remains.

To Dr. Birch and C. T. Newton, Esq., of the British Museum, who kindly gave every facility for the measurement of the antiquities in their charge, my best thanks are due; as also to H. W. Chisholm, Esq., the Warden of the Standards, for his kindness in having carefully compared a standard scale of Kater's which I had employed.

W. M. FLINDERS PETRIE.

Bromley, Kent.

CONTENTS.

———◦◇◦———

		PAGE
PREFACE		v
INTRODUCTION		1

CHAPTER I. METHODS OF INDUCTIVE EXAMINATION.

(1) Object to be attained by inductive examination . . 9
(2) 1st method, by ratios of pairs of measures . . . 9
(3) 2nd method, by ratios of groups of measures . . . 11
(4) 3rd method, by ratios of one group to all others . . 12
(5) 4th method, by ratios of differences of measures . . 12
(6) Ascertaining the usual multiplication, &c., of the unit of measure 14
(7) Multiples and fractions that are likely to be found in use 15
(8) Long lengths unsuited for examination 16
(9) Simple multiples of unit found instead of unit. Many multiples and fractions often in use, as in England . 17
(10) Least number of measures that is sufficient . . . 19
(11) Grouping of similar units together, to obtain the mean unit 19
(12) Three classes of probable opinions on the subject . . 21
(13) Probability of fallacies, and the means of checking them 22

CHAPTER II. APPLICATION OF THE DOCTRINE OF PROBABILITIES.

(14) Explanation of the term probable error 24
(15) Probable error a fallible statement. Infinite series of probable errors 25
(16) Formulæ for obtaining probable error 26
(17) Weighting of observations 28
(18) Example of ascertaining unit, and its probable error . 28

PAGE

(19) Probabilities of multiples of the probable error . . 30
(20) Correct theories of weighting contiguous spaces . . 31
(21) Practical application of them 32
(22) Appreciation of methods as important as their rigorous application 35
(23) Averages and weighted means applicable in different cases 36

CHAPTER III. SOURCES OF ERROR, NOTES ON ASCERTAINING UNITS, AND RESULTS TO BE EXPECTED.

(24) Probable error results from workmanship and measurement 38
(25) Apparent accuracy in measurements often fallacious . 39
(26) Different units may be found in contiguous work of different dates 41
(27) Original scheme of building is to be noticed . . . 42
(28) Accuracy of workmanship 43
(29) Real and approximate ratios between units . . . 44
(30) Number of units found. Analogy of Continental metrology 45

CHAPTER IV. EGYPT.

(31) Plan of arrangement 47
(32) Unit of ·4350 inches 48
(33) „ ·5020 „ × 50 = 25·10 Royal Persian cubit 48
(34) . „ ·6766 „ × 16 = 10·82 Plinian foot . 49
(35) „ 20·64 „ Royal Egyptian cubit . . . 50
(36) „ 2·111 „ 51
(37) „ 21·40 „ Assyrian cubit 51
(38) „ 1·547 „ × 8 = 12·376 Olympic foot . 52
(39) Units of 13·19, 1·736, and 9·46 ; Drusian, ⅛ Philetairean, and Pythic feet 52
(40) Units of ·7276, ·7387, and ·7491 inches. Digits . . 53
(41) Conclusions from the variations of the digits . . . 55
(42) The digit a fixed standard 57
(43) Table of inductive results from Egyptian measures . 59
(44) Cubits, &c., marked on the ancient cubit rods . . 59

PAGE

(45) Identity of these with units found inductively . . 61
(46) Normal length of Egyptian sceptres, &c., in canon of
       proportion 63

CHAPTER V. BABYLONIA, ASSYRIA, PERSIA, AND SYRIA.

(47) Assyrian unit of ·7300 inches. The digit . . . 65
(48)   „   „   20·60 Babylonian cubit . . . 65
(49)   „   „   19·97 Half of Great U . . . 66
(50)   „   „   25·28 Royal cubit 66
(51)   „   „   1·189 × 8 = 9·62, Pythic foot . . 67
(52) Units found by Dr. Oppert; unit of 21·37 from inscrip-
       tion; table of results 67
(53) Persian unit of 1·013 or 25·34. The Royal Persian
                              cubit 69
(54)   „   „   20·70 Babylonian cubit . . . 70
(55)   „   „   1·730 Duodecimal of Babylonian cubit 71
(56)   „   ·„   16·88 71
(57)   „   ·„   7·339 or 10 digits 72
(58)   „   „   ·7652 × 25 = 19·13 Double Pythic
                              foot 72
(59)   „   „   21·375 Assyrian cubit 72
(60) Table of Persian results 73
(61) Syrian unit of ·721 to ·740. The digit . . . 73
(62)   „   „   3·305⎫ ¼ Drusian foot 74
(63)   „   „   3·333⎭
(64)   „   „   4·049 ⅕ Assyrian U 75
(65)   „   „   25·2 Sacred Hebrew cubit . . . 75
(66)   „   „   1·113 (1/10 Phœnician foot) . . . 76
(67)   „   „   1·427 76
(68)   „   „   11·67 Roman foot 76
(69)   „   „   20·73 Egyptian cubit 76
(70) Table of Syrian results 76

CHAPTER VI. ASIA MINOR AND GREECE.

(71) Asia Minor unit of 20·64   The Egypto-Samian cubit . 78
(72)   „   „   17·25   from   „   „ . 79
(73)   „   „   ·7330 digit 79
(74)   „   „   5·658⎫ 1·885 80
(75)   „   „   1·884⎭

PAGE

(76) Asia Minor unit of 10·91 Plinian foot . . . 81
(77)   „   „ 13·36 Drusian foot . . . 81
(78)   „   „ 3·994 $\frac{1}{10}$ Assyrian Great U . . 81
(79)   „   „ 12·11 Olympic foot . . . 82
(80)   „   „ 11·64 Roman foot . . . 82
(81)   „   „ 19·30 Double Pythic foot . . 83
(82)   „   „ 1·791⎫ 8·95 83
(83)   „   „ 2·235⎭
(84) Table of Asia Minor results 84
(85) Greek unit of 11·60 The Pelasgo-Etrurio-Roman foot . 85
(86) „   „ 12·40 Babylonian foot 86
(87) „   „ 12·16 Olympic foot 87
(88) „   „ 1·131 87
(89) „ units of 6·43 and 6·63, $\frac{2}{3}$ Pythic foot and $\frac{1}{2}$
     Drusian foot 88
(90) Greek unit of 2·538 $\frac{1}{10}$ Royal Persian cubit . . 89
(91) „   „ 17·88 89
(92) Table of Greek results 89
(93) Decimal scales used in Greece, and original length of digit 90

CHAPTER VII. ITALY, AFRICA, AND SARDINIA.

(94) Italian unit of 23·05 Etruria 93
(95) Roman „ 12·45 The Babylonian foot . . . 94
(96) „   „ 11·68 Roman foot 95
(97) „   „ 7·32 10 digits 96
(98) „   „ 12·19 Olympic foot 96
(99) „   „ 13·45 Drusian foot 97
(100) „   „ 4·27 $\frac{1}{5}$ Assyrian cubit . . . 97
(101) „   „ 1·996 $\frac{1}{20}$ Assyrian Great U . . 97
(102) „   „ ·7500 Long digit 98
(103) Isolated units only once found 98
(104) Table of Italian results, including Roman colonies . 98
(105) African unit of 13·34 Drusian foot 99
(106) „   „ 11·16 (Phœnician foot) . . . 99
(107) „ units of 11·74 and 9·62. Roman and Pythic feet 100
(108) Sardinian unit of 1·384 (× 8 = Phœnician foot) . 100
(109) „   „ 3·399 100
(110) „   „ 19·74 101

PAGE

(111) Sardinian unit of   1·896   ⅛ Pythic foot   .   .   . 101

(112)   ,,   ,,   10·80   ½ Assyrian cubit   .   . 101

(113)   ,,   units of   20·08, 29·53, and 13·26;   ½ U, 10

      palms, and Drusian foot   101

(114) Table of Sardinian results   102

CHAPTER VIII. MEDIÆVAL IRELAND AND ENGLAND.

(115) Irish unit of 4·46   103

(116)   ,,   ,,   5·67   103

(117)   ,,   ,,   5·34   104

(118)   ,,   ,,   4·27   104

(119) Unison of these units in a unit of 21·34   .   .   . 104

(120) Unit of 4·89   105

(121) Isolated Irish units   105

(122) English unit of   ·9998. Early English inch ($\frac{1}{40}$ Great U) 105

(123)   ,,   ,,   13·22   (Drusian foot)   .   . 107

(124)   ,,   ,,   12·47   (Babylonian foot) .   . 107

(125)   ,,   ,,   7·80   108

(126)   ,,   ,,   12·97   108

(127)   ,,   ,,   7·96   (⅛ of Great U) .   .   . 108

(128)   ,,   ,,   11·60   (Roman foot) .   .   . 109

(129)   ,,   ,,   8·46   109

(130)   ,,   ,,   6·87   109

(131)   ,,   ,,   12·17   (Olympic foot) .   .   . 109

(132) Unclassed English units   110

(133) Table of English results, and origin of English units   . 110

CHAPTER IX. RUDE STONE REMAINS, AMERICA, INDIA, &c.

(134) Remarks on the character of Pre-historic remains   . 112

(135) Instances of their metrical character   .   .   . 113

(136) British unit of 21·38   (Assyrian cubit ?)   .   . 114

(137)   ,,   ,,   22·51   (Phœnician foot ?)   .   . 115

(138)   ,,   ,,   20·41   117

(139)   ,,   ,,   4·70   117

(140)   ,,   ,,   3·29   117

(141)   ,,   ,,   15·95   (⅖ Great U ?) .   .   . 118

(142)   ,,   ,,   11·66   (Roman foot ?) .   .   . 118

PAGE

(143) Danish unit of 12·80 Runic remains 119

(144) Table of Pre-historic results. Remarks and details . 119

(145) Unit of 2·92, Jutland, palm 121

(146) Units of 66·7 Africa, and 15·58 Sinai 121

(147) „ 4·94 and 8·40 Ogham stones . . . 121

(148) Geometrical character of some N. American earthworks 122

(149) Unit of 12·60 used in American earthworks . . . 123

(150) Same unit used in portable remains of the mound-builders 123

(151) Unit of 10·65 in Mexico 124

(152) „ 6·70 in Central America 125

(153) „ 44·6 in Polynesia 125

(154) „ 17·82 in India⎫ . . 125

(155) „ 8·33 „ ⎬ Elora temples . . 126

(156) „ 6·93 „ ⎭ . . 126

(157) „ 18·38 „ Rude stone remains in Dekhan 126

(158) Table of Indian results 127

(159) Unit of 6·116 in Ceylon 127

(160) Connections of Indian units 128

(161) Length of the Ilahi gaz; 34·09 by Abul Fazl . . 128

(162) Table of early Mohammedan units in India . . . 129

(163) Turkish unit of 11·63 Roman foot 130

(164) „ „ 3·014 130

(165) Persian unit of 1·016 Ancient Persian $\frac{1}{25}$ of cubit . 130

(166) „ „ 12·42 Babylonian foot . . . 131

(167) „ „ 16·89 131

(168) „ „ 13·68 131

(169) Table of Turkish and Persian results 131

CHAPTER X. SYNOPSIS OF THE INDUCTIVE EXAMINATION.
HISTORY OF METRICAL UNITS.

(170) Forms and derivatives of the 25·15 unit or Sacred cubit . 133

(171) „ „ ·729 „ or digit . 136

(172) „ „ 20·63 „ or Egyptian cubit . 138

(173) „ of the 21·38 unit, or Assyrian cubit . . 140

(174) „ 13·22 „ or Drusian foot . . 140

PAGE

(175) Forms of the 10·85 unit, or Plinian foot . . 140
(176) „ 13·89 „ or Philetairean foot . . 141
(177) „ 11·17 „ or Phœnician foot . . 141
(178) „ 17·88 „ or Aryan unit . . . 141
(179) Other units 141
(180) Original length of the principal metrical standards . 142
(181) Synoptical table of all the units of measure obtained . 142

GENERAL RESULTS.

(182) Mean error of workmanship in different countries . 143
(183) Details of the additions to metrology attempted or
     achieved, and general summary 144
(184) Farther researches suggested 150
List of Books from which measurements have been extracted 152

INTRODUCTION.

THE materials for a history of measures have been principally, if not wholly, derived from the statements of ancient authors, and the use of monumental data has been confined to the elucidation and support of these literary remains. The object of this essay is to point out the means by which the independent and complete evidence of ancient monuments may be obtained, apart from any other sources of information. The literary statements on ancient metrology, therefore, obtain less notice here than that which is really due to them in a complete view of the subject, because they have been already so fully examined, and have had so many deductions drawn from them.

" By induction is to be understood the process of collecting general truths from the examination of particular facts."* Inductive metrology accordingly ascertains the " general truths" of the units of measure in use, from the " particular facts" of those multiples of measures which ancient remains preserve to us.

So far as this method of examination has been worked, the results, though placing many facts in a somewhat new light, have not been opposed to any of the recognised canons of metrology; but are clearly in agreement

---

* Whewell, Hist. Induct. Sciences, I. 6.

with what may be called the *literary* metrology in all its
principal elements.

The historical sciences seem to pass through two stages
in the course of their development—the literary and
the monumental—the deductive and the inductive.   In
the first, the science is based on such information as has
descended to us by means of literature ; and the principal method of advancement is by deductions, combi-
nations of the stated facts, and criticism of the internal
evidence.   In the second stage, monuments are the
principal basis of the science ; and literary evidence
serves only for filling up such vacancies, and for making
such connections, as those remains do not supply.   In
Egyptian and Assyrian history the Greek historians
furnished us with the first stage, but now we look to the
monuments as the primary authority.   So it has been
in ethnology and philology, where the monument of
language, whenever available, has supplanted the statements of the ancient authors.   So it will probably be
in metrology ; and when the tale of each monument
shall have been read, the vague and often debatable
language of the ancients, having served its day, will
be justly regarded as more a matter of curiosity than of
use.

In such a well-known subject as metrology, that so
little requires the results of modern science for its development, it may seem strange that there should still
remain any fresh methods of inquiry.   But it is with
this as with many other branches of knowledge, taking
the oft-used simile of the tree of science, the branches
have grown forward so vigorously as to leave many buds
undeveloped.

Perhaps in this essay rather more credit may be

given to some of the ancients, with regard to their care and design in building, than is usually allowed to them during the present reaction, caused by the rapid advance of modern science. Our subject, however, has nothing to do with astronomical temples, solar systems of the ancients, or mystic or scientific meanings in ancient remains; but merely recognises that in most ages, when men have to lay out or plan any work that requires to be alike on two sides, if they have a measure they will use it; and they will probably use whole numbers in preference to fractions, and round numbers in preference to uneven ones, merely for convenience in their work. Some nations, such as the Aryan Hindûs, have, moreover, an inherent love of metricality which induces them to pay attention to measures; and others are led to give the same care by their desire to produce regularity of work, or by their attention to recognised canons of proportion. Though this essay is thus based upon postulates that probably few would be found to deny; yet this subject, like many others, might easily be rendered absurd and useless, by encumbering it with an undue regard to every mere coincidence irrespective of sense and method.

When a unit of measure has once been lost to literature, it can never be recovered by the use of the present methods, since the only use hitherto made of monuments has been to corroborate the *known* instead of discovering the unknown; and thus when literature is in any case deficient, metrology is supposed to have never existed. That the most civilised peoples had units of measure, and that the lowest savages have none, is about all that is as yet definitely known; and the boundary of the use of measures is quite undefined, or, worse still, assumed without evidence. But that units of measure are used by semi-savage nations is shown by the Tahitians, who were wholly ignorant of any writing or current symbolic marks, and who yet had a recognised unit of measure.[*] The identity of the dimensions of many North American earthworks has been very reasonably concluded by Squier (who has examined them more than any one else) to prove the existence of a unit of measure; and this is further corroborated by the ten copper bracelets of exactly equal weight (whatever accuracy that indefinite statement may have) which were found in the Scioto valley. An ethnologist[†] has declared, in the face of these facts, that the mound-builders could not have had a balance or a standard of length, because such instruments are above the culture of that people. This is assuming the very point in question; and, to take the explanation of the equal earthworks that he offers us— namely, that a long cord and a bundle of stakes will suffice to lay out " any earthwork of the mound-builders, and to copy in new places a work already constructed"— this very supposition, that care would be bestowed on exactly reproducing the dimensions of any earthwork, implies such an attention to measure and size as we cannot suppose to exist without producing, or being the product of, the use of a definite standard. That this was not a passing freak, or an accident, is undoubted, from the same length occurring in a dozen or more earthworks mentioned by Squier in Ohio, Indiana, and New York, thus ranging over hundreds of miles of country. Farther evidence on the amount of design shown by the

[*] Hawkesworth's Voyages, II. 228.
[†] Tylor in 3rd Session International Congress Prehistoric Archæology; Wallace, however, in his address to the British Association, 1876, agrees with Squier.

mound-builders is adduced where their works are specially examined in the following pages (sect. 148).

In more civilised communities, the importance attached to measures is well known ; for instance, in that early Egyptian work, the " Book of the Dead," the soul pleads, " I have not shortened the cubit ;" and among the Jews, the Levites were appointed to attend to "all manner of measure and size," referring respectively to liquid measure and linear size, as is clear in the original.

On this question of the existence of standards of measure in the various grades of civilisation, as well as on the origin and distribution of units, it is only sought in this essay to subject assumptions to proof, where such can be obtained ; and not to rest satisfied with making suppositions, when the evidences of the subject are at our disposal. Even if the evidence be not in all cases convincing, it, at least, is evidence, and *any* evidence will more than balance *no* evidence.

The "speechless past" which has been so often deplored, has, in its monuments, a voice; to which we may hope that inductive metrology, when developed, will give clear interpretation ; and just as comparative philology has revealed to us much of the origin and history of races, so comparative metrology may reveal much of the history and origin of monuments and their builders. When a general network of information shall have been obtained, by ascertaining the units, and their variations, used in different times and places ; we may be enabled, by our observations on a structure, to fix its place in ethnology and history. A recent authority on the subject* has ventured still farther in his expectations of the

---

* Don Vasquez Quiepo.

future of metrology; and with a vast amount of research we may hope to see his prognostications fulfilled. But the present state of our knowledge is but elementary, and hitherto only the most authorised units of a small number of countries have been known.

With regard to the following pages of results, it may be asked why some of the stores of measures in many well-known books, have not been worked upon. But it would be the labour of a lifetime to carry this subject to anything like completion, or to any state in which its deficiencies would not be as striking as its results. In this essay the aim has been to select samples for examination from several countries, in order to try the plan of induction thoroughly; and also by this means to cover as wide a field with tolerably correct results, as was possible in a few years.

All the methods and results have been stated concisely, and in such a form as seemed most useful for further examinations; a principal object being to give the amount of evidence for each result, and also to enable any one to check the results by referring to the original list of measures, and trying them with the unit obtained from them. To have given all the measures, and the number of units in each length, would have produced a monstrous mass of figures and letterpress such as few would wade through; the chances of a book being read being probably in inverse proportion to the square of its length; and it is hoped that the amount of authority for each result arrived at, will be sufficiently clear to those who care to examine it.

Doubts and difficulties have not been slighted or left unnoticed, but in all dubious questions the uncertainty of them is acknowledged and discussed. No attempt has been made to try to obtain the acquiescence of others by ignoring uncertainties. It has been well said that "The reader is easily led captive by a writer who has no hesitation;" but this stolen consent is an agreement that snaps with the first shock; whereas, when difficulties and uncertainties have been faced from the beginning, they are not reckoned at more than their true value.

CHAPTER I.

METHODS OF INDUCTIVE EXAMINATION.

(1) IN all monuments planned by means of a standard of measure, we have a series of unknown multiples of an unknown unit. As the unknown multiples are, however, usually integral numbers (or simple relations of such) in all lengths under about ten or twenty feet, and simple multiples of integral numbers in the longer lengths; we have a limitation, by means of which the unknown multiples and unit of measure may be ascertained.

There are three or four modes of working this question, all nearly related, but each of rather a different nature; and in practice it is best to take a modification of all of them, suited to the case in hand. The direct object, of course, is to obtain the value of the ancient unit in terms of the British inch, or such other standard as the measurements have been stated in by modern travellers or others. All the methods depend on the plan of ascertaining every likely ratio between pairs of the measured lengths; and then comparing these ratios, to find which of them may be combined so as to give a simple number to each length, that shall represent the probable number of the original units by which that length is formed—*i.e.*, the multiples of the unit used by the original designer.

(2) This may be done by noting all likely ratios of

successive pairs of measures, and observing what ratio will result from them all. For an example, take the following measures of the Cypriote tablet from Dali, in the British Museum :—

Parts measured.	Inches.	Approximate ratios of pairs of the measures.*			Number of units.
		†	†	†	
Height of panel . .	44·2	7 12 13 22½			60
Width across pilasters	25·49	4 7 7½ 13			35
„ „ „	25·49		26 17½		35
Height of stylobate .	2·92		3 2		4
„ „ „	2·92		2		1
Height of architrave	1·45		1		2
„ „ „	1·45			2	2
Height of abaci . .	2·15			3	3
„ „ „	2·15			2	3
Width of plinths . .	3·24			3	4½
„ „ „	3·24			4½ 7	4½
Height of plinths . .	5·77			8 12½	8

Here 44·2 : 25·49 inches : : 7 : 4, also as 12 : 7, as 13 : 7½, and as 22½ : 13; these are all bracketed together as being alternative ratios. Next 25·49 : 2·92 inches : : 26 : 3, also as 17½ : 2; these are the only likely ratios. Next 2·92 : 1·45 inches : : 2 : 1; and there is no other ratio likely. Similarly the other columns show the ratios existing between the other quantities. The last column is a combination of the preceding ratios; the numbers being those which occur in the preceding ratios, or else doubles or other simple multiples of such; selecting such ratios (marked †) from the bracketed alternatives as agreed best with the other ratios.

---

* These ratios are quickly obtained by simple inspection of the slide rule.

This last column accordingly gives the only series of simple numbers which bear the same ratio to each other, as do the measured lengths respectively opposite to them; and therefore all these numbers bear the same ratio to their respective measured lengths. Thus we are justified in assuming that if a unit of measure was used, there were 60 of these units in the 44·2 inches, 35 in the 25·49 inches, and so on; so that these numbers are its respective multipliers employed by the original designer of the monument.

(3) The second method is to group together all measures which are seen at a glance to be evidently related, and then to search for ratios between these groups. Thus, using the above measures, we see at the first glance that 1·45, 2·92, and 5·77 inches are very nearly doubles of each other, standing to each other as 1, 2, and 4. Again, 2·15 : 3·24 inches : : 2 : 3, which is very apparent. Again, 1·45 : 2·15 inches : : 2 : 3. Thus from these ratios, which are evident at first sight, we should obtain the following numbers to represent the probable multiples :—

Inches.				
1·45	1	2		2
2·92	2			4
5·77	4			8
2·15		3	2	3
3·24			3	4½

And then continuing this last column, and applying it to the remaining measures, they will of course have the same numbers against them as in the preceding method. The above case is a very simple one; but often it happens in a numerous series of measures, that several groups of four or five measures each are apparent, and the connection between them has to be sought.

(4) The third method is analogous to the above, and rather quicker. By looking through the measures, and selecting those which will easily and simply form the most numerous group, we have a tolerable certainty that the group consists of anciently *measured* quantities, and not chance lengths; and that in these cases the multiples of the unit are some simple numbers. Therefore, taking the base of this largest group—in the Dali tablet, 1·45 inches—as a standard, the ratios of all the other measures to this one are noted: and the number that most frequently occurs on its side of the ratios is presumably the unit's multiple belonging to it.

Thus

Inches.					2	2½	8½	1	9	
1·45	1	1	2	2	2	2½	8½	1	9	2
2·92	2									4
5·77		4								8
2·15			3							3
3·24				4½						4½
25·49					35	44	150			35
44·2								30	275	60

Here 2 (or its half, 1) occurs as the ratio number to 1·45 inches in every case where there is no alternative; and also in each of the groups of alternative cases. Thus the numbers in the final column will give the original multiples of the unit used.

(5) The fourth method differs considerably from each of the preceding, and is often useful in difficult cases; it consists in taking the differences of the measured quantities, and then taking the oftenest-recurring difference as a basis (like 1·45 inches in Method 3), or else searching for a harmonizing ratio for these diffe-

rences. The advantage of this method is that the quantities to be treated, are thus much lower multiples of the unit, and consequently the ratio between them is easier found, and is often evident at a glance. Short lengths are not so easily reduced to the unit as the differences of long lengths, because fractions are often introduced in short lengths; whereas in long lengths, the multiples being generally integral numbers, their differences are also integral numbers of units.

The Dali tablet is not suitable as an example of this method, because the lengths are so short that the preceding methods are more applicable. As an example we may take the porch of Chideock Church, Dorsetshire; the measures are—

	Inches.	Differences.	Units.
Radius of sun-dial	6·9 ...	6·9	... 1
Side of door moulding to side of		32·8	
porch	40·7 ...	7·0	... 6
Side of doorway to side of porch .	47·7 ...	6·9	... 7
Door wide	54·6 ...	20·0	... 8
Stone arching blocks over door, wide	74·6 ...	75·4	... 11
Whole width of porch . . .	150·0 ...		... 22

Here we see the same amount (6·9 or 7·0 inches) repeated three times over in the differences; and taking this hint, by adopting this as a base, we find that the measures agree pretty closely to it; the multiples being given in the last column.

Of course the small internal errors will appear far larger in proportion on the difference than on the whole; and sometimes a double error (*i.e.*, a + error in one measure and a − error in the next) will thus be thrown on a difference of only a few inches, and appear monstrous, when it would be quite unobtrusive on the whole measures of several feet in length. This method, though quick, and easily applied without a slide rule, is not to be worked with such care as the others; and if in any case the differences are not seen to group well, it may be discarded as unsuitable in that instance.*

(6) Having by one of these methods obtained the original multiples of the unit employed (and therefore of course the unit itself), the multiples should be examined to see if many of them are divisible by any integral number.

For instance, the multiples used in the north door of Maiden Newton Church, Dorsetshire, are 45, 84, 9, and 8. Now 3 enters into three of these multiples, 45, 84, and 9, ÷ 3 being 15, 28, and 3; thus we may presume that 3 or 6 of these units formed a *super-unit*, as it might be termed; just as 3 feet form a yard, and 4 × 3 inches form the foot, in the modern English series. The south door of the same church (of a very different date) was built with a different unit, and its multiples are 2, 2½, 4, 40, 45, 50, and 55. Here 5 enters into most of the multiples; and accordingly 5 or 10 of these units formed the *super-unit*, the system being decimal, like that of the metre.

Conversely we may often find that fractions of a unit were used; for instance, in the multiples of the Aqueduct of Hadrian, at Athens, there occur 5½, 5⅓, 3⅓, 2⅓, and 3½. From these we must conclude that the unit was ÷ 6, or perhaps ÷ 12, like our foot.

The best way of ascertaining how a unit was divided, is to reduce all the short lengths to decimal fractions of the unit found; very often the division is plain imme-

* For example, the multiples of the unit might be 1½, 7, 12, 21, 25, and 32; and the differences, therefore, would be 5½, 5, 9, 4, and 7 units; and the ratio between these differences would not be very apparent.

diately; but if hidden by bad measures, or unmetrical quantities, it can generally be seen by putting the fractions down in a rough diagram.

(7) A most important point to be attended to, is the character of the numbers assumed as multiples. Of course numbers may be found to fit *any* given measures, but it would be very unlikely that uneven or prime numbers (except the lowest) would be taken as multiples. All integral numbers up to 20 may be fairly expected to have been used, and also those numbers $\times$ 2 or 4. Also such multiples as 21, 25, 27, 35, 42, &c. Twenty-two and 26 might perhaps be considered unlikely multiples, but they are expressly given as principal measures in the still-existing specification of Catterick Church, A.D. 1412; and in the same document lengths of 70, 11, 16, and 44 feet are mentioned. Such multiples, however, as 47, 53, 59, &c., would be decidedly unlikely, and should accordingly not be depended on to explain measures.

Of course such fractions as $\frac{1}{8}$, $\frac{1}{6}$, $\frac{1}{5}$, $\frac{1}{4}$, $\frac{1}{3}$, &c., may be fairly expected to occur in short lengths; and some multiples that seem unlikely at first sight may be intentional; such as $5\frac{1}{3}$ (*i.e.*, $16 \div 3$), $6\frac{2}{3}$ ($20 \div 3$), $8\frac{1}{3}$ ($25 \div 3$), $41\frac{2}{3}$ ($250 \div 6$), $62\frac{1}{2}$ ($250 \div 4$), and many others which need not be mentioned. These numbers may easily occur, either from an equal division of a space into 3, 4, or 6 parts, or from the unit being subdivided duodecimally or binarily; just as an English building might be principally planned in round numbers of yards, though having some lengths of, say, 70 feet ($23\frac{1}{3}$ yards), or 80 feet ($26\frac{2}{3}$ yards).

In searching for the original unit of measure, a subdivided length, such as a façade, is useful, especially if subdivided in more than one way : since it is clear that after deducing the number of units, according to each of the methods of division, the sum of the multiples should be similar in all ways in which the space is divided, and should probably be an even number. Thus at St. Catherine's Chapel, Guildford, the division of one end is in equal $\frac{1}{3}$rds ; and on the other end the spaces are relatively as 6 : 10 : 13 : 16, the sum of which is 45 ; this gives such a likely number of units (15) to each of the thirds at the other end, that it adds much to the evidence for the use of such a unit in this case.

(8) A point which seems to have been misapprehended, in some attempts at obtaining units inductively, is the probability of round numbers in planning long lengths. *Long lengths are of little value for obtaining the unit.* I confess to having thought just the opposite at first ; but after extracting some hundreds of units, from all sorts of materials, accurate and rough, I am forced to this conclusion. The moderately short lengths, from about two to twenty feet, are the most useful material. In these the errors of work and measurement are not such as ever to obscure the number of units ; and yet the number is also generally free from small fractions. In long lengths, on the contrary, the errors may amount to a foot or more, and thus produce some uncertainty as to the number of units, even if the unit be already tolerably known. Again, there is such a choice of likely multiples of nearly equal quantity in many cases as to produce much uncertainty. It is often hard to say whether a length is intended for 95 or 96 units ; between 62$\frac{1}{2}$, 64, 65, and 66$\frac{2}{3}$, again, we may be uncertain ; 70 and 72, and 108 and 110, and many other likely numbers, are so near that it is hard to settle (without some sub-

division of the space) how many units it may contain, unless the accuracy of both the work and the measures can be well trusted.

Also a compound length may not be a round number at all, but may consist of such numbers as $15+2+7\frac{1}{2}+2+15=41\frac{1}{2}$ units, or $8+6+9+6+8=37$ units, or an internal space of 72 units + 2 end walls of 5 units thickness=82 units; all of these would be likely, say in a divided façade; and if the architect thought more of the proportions of his work than of making the total lengths round numbers, some such result would be very probable.*

(9) After what has been remarked above on the subdivisions and multiples of units, and the method of obtaining the units, it is plain that often a simple multiple or fraction of the unit will be arrived at by these methods instead of the main unit; just as the inch or yard might be deduced from a building mainly planned in feet, if inches were often introduced, or if triple multiples of feet were favoured by the architect. Also, when there are only a few lengths on which to work, it may easily happen that a half or double or third of the unit may be obtained; as a considerable collection of measures is required to see what length of unit will treat its multiples

---

* In Dr. Oppert's use of the Persepolitan long lengths (Etalons Assyriennes) he has deduced from them a unit which will not explain any of the dozens of shorter measures of the same buildings, owing to his supposing that the main lengths must be simple decimal multiples of the unit. This is enough to make us doubt the result, even if the unit thus obtained did not vary so greatly as it is supposed to do ; to fit the measures (which are good ones) the unit is required to vary as much as a whole inch on its length of $21\frac{1}{2}$ inches. It is necessary to notice this to explain how it is that units are found in this essay by inductive examination (each building being treated separately) which are different from that stated by Dr. Oppert.

and fractions in the best way. For instance, in a building we may find a unit whose multiples are 2, 3, and 10;
but other measures of the same building may also give
us 32 and 64 as multiples. If so, it is more likely that
the unit was larger, and the multiples really $\frac{1}{2}$, $\frac{3}{4}$, $2\frac{1}{2}$, 8,
and 16; or they might be $\frac{1}{4}$, $\frac{3}{8}$, $1\frac{1}{4}$, 4, and 8 almost as
well. Eighty-one would be unlikely as a multiple of a
unit; but if there are no $\frac{1}{3}$rds among the multiples of
this same unit, all of them may be $\div$ 3, (and the unit
accordingly $\times$ 3), and then 27 (81 $\div$ 3) would not be
unlikely.

This must be remembered when considering the
results given farther on. It might be objected against
them, that it is seldom the same unit is found in all the
instances given; as in the groups of units supposed to be
identical, many require multiplying or dividing by some
simple numbers before they will all give the same result.
Now it is clear from the above remarks that if the materials are not abundant, it is very likely that a multiple, or
sub-multiple, of the original unit will be obtained instead
of it; and, beside this, multiples or sub-multiples of the
units were very likely to be used as bases in planning
work, as well as the main unit. Inches, feet, and yards
might all be used as independent units in English architecture of the same date and place; 12ths, 10ths, and
8ths of an inch are all common divisions, and might be
equally well used; to say nothing of nails or hands, both
of which are parts of the same English system. *Accurate coincidence of length* is a truer test of the connection
of two units than simplicity of connecting multiples. A
line is the 27th of a nail, and yet they are both parts of
one system of measures, that of the foot and inch; and
though it may be said that in England no one would

think of using a nail or a line as a unit of measure; yet the case is very different in countries where want of communication and of federal government, leaves each locality free to follow out its own idiosyncrasies, unchecked by its dissimilarity with surrounding communities.

(10) The least number of measures that will suffice for ascertaining the unit is three, or possibly two. The measure of one length may prove the absence of any particular unit; two if sufficiently accurate, might suffice to show the unit; three will generally (if suitable multiples) give a unit with tolerable certainty. For instance, the following sarcophagus, or rather cist, found at Jerusalem, near the Convent of the Cross (Palestine Exploration statement) :—

	Inches.		Units.		Unit, in inches.
Long . . .	30·9	=	5	×	6·18
Wide . . .	12·4	=	2	×	6·20
High . . .	15·5	=	$2\frac{1}{2}$	×	6·20

Thus the unit is, practically speaking, certain to be 6·19 inches, or perhaps half or double of this.

The number of measures from which each unit in the following pages has been deduced, is mentioned in every case before the name of the subject : several more measures of a less accurate character were generally examined as well; but only those employed for taking the mean value of the unit have been counted. The uncertainty of those units deduced from only two or three lengths, is sufficiently manifest without farther notice ; and they are only given as suggestions, which may be corroborated by other buildings and remains.

(11) After the units have been thus ascertained as nearly as may be, the next step is to group together

those units in any one country and age that are identical, or that seem to be derived from one another; and then from them deduce the mean value of the unit, hereafter called the *mean unit.*

It is not proposed to give any value to a unit which seems to have no connection with any others. Such may be merely accidental, perhaps from some chance unit adopted by the builder for lack of a better; and the greater number of the results of mere casual coincidences will also be found among the unconnected units. Such ungrouped units are merely mentioned as possibilities which may obtain corroboration.

Fallacies will occur in the grouping, as well as in the extraction of units from the measured lengths; they will, however, affect but a small proportion of the whole results, and therefore must be tolerated for the sake of the true information: in time they will be gradually weeded out, as more materials are collected and classified; for every science has to confess to mistakes and amended conclusions.

The grouping of units requires some attention. In treating the units of Asia Minor, for instance, every likely ratio of connection between the units has been noted, pairing them in every possible manner; these groups of connections thus formed have been mapped off with the probable errors of the units, and every unit which seemed to belong to more than one group has been examined; first, to see if any of the separate groups of units were likely to belong in reality to one mean unit, and could be amalgamated; and if not, to see with which group each of the few undecided units would best agree. For this end their multiples were considered; for instance, if a unit required to be ÷ 3 to fit the majority of a given group, and if the multiples of it in the building in which it was used had some ⅓rds among them, then it was very likely to belong to that group: if, however, there were no ⅓rds, but, on the contrary, multiples of 3, such as 27 or 63, it was more likely to belong to another group; for if the *mean unit* were used in the building, these multiples of 3 would have a further multiplication by 3; which would be unlikely, as it would result in 81 and 189 as multiple numbers. Also the locality was considered somewhat in a few cases where the grouping of a unit seemed uncertain. The Egyptian units were worked very similarly; and those of other countries on the same principles, though, not being so numerous or intricate, they did not require the same details.

Thus it is sought to combine together for one mean result, all those units which were simple derivatives of the same original; or which have been accidentally multiplied or divided by some simple number, such as 2, 3, 4, or 10, in the process of extracting them from their multiples preserved to us in ancient buildings.

(12) There are three different views that will probably be taken of this subject. First, that all the methods and conclusions are fallacious, and that we can only trust to literary information. This (which may be called the George Cornewall Lewis view) is sufficiently refuted by the fact that more than half the results exactly tally with our literary information, and that none contradict it.

The second view is more important to consider, as it will probably be more usual than the preceding: it is that the results which agree with information otherwise obtained from literary sources, &c., are correct; but that all results which are not forestalled by, or at least to be expected from, our present knowledge, are merely the product of casual coincidences, and have no relation to the original units of measure.

The third view is that only a small proportion of the results are fallacious ; and that these are, by subsequent grouping of the units, either eradicated by their not agreeing with any group, or else so far checked as not to seriously affect the truth in any way. This is the view to which I have been led from working these methods, in extracting the various units detailed in this essay.

With regard to the second view, it should be observed that the few new units found, stand on just as good a monumental basis as those previously known, and in some cases (as the 12·40 foot of Greece and Rome, and the 5·65 and 8·95 of Asia Minor) on a far better basis ; the evidence for them is of precisely the same nature, and is often so clear that the conclusion is unavoidable ; and farther, those monuments from which they are re-covered will not agree in any way to any recognized unit.

(13) After extracting some 600 units from measures of various qualities, I am inclined to consider that not 1 in 10 of these units is the result of fortuitous coinci-dence, and perhaps 1 in 20 or 30 might be a fair con-clusion : estimating this by the frequency (or rather rarity) with which cases turn up, where each of two or more distinct and unrelated units, would seem to satisfy all the measures ; since the proportion of fallacies being certainly small, the frequency of two ratios fitting the same measures will about show the proportion of falla-cious results in the whole quantity.

Judging thus, 1 in 10 is probably an over-estimate, but to make certain we will assume 1 in 5 to be fallacious.

If so, it is 1 in 25 that any given pair of units are both fallacious, and 1 in 125, 600, or 3,000 that a group of 3, 4, or 5 units related to each other should be all fallacious. It is therefore evident what great improbabilities there are, of a mean unit, the result of a coinciding group, being a mere casual coincidence. Not only so, but this also shows how little likely the casual coincidences are to affect the mean units to which they may be supposed to belong. And besides the improbability of their falling together in one group, it must be remembered that they will in most cases have larger errors than the genuine original units ; and thus as the weight that each has in determining the mean depends on its error, the fortuitous results (even apart from their scarcity) will but little affect the mean units. Also the false units would seldom fall casually into a group of real units, so as to be included among them.

Thus though there is a certainty of a portion of these units being fictitious, and having no relation to the original unit employed (if there were any such in these cases), yet by the system of combining the similar units together into means, extending over some hundreds of years and of miles, we may rest assured that errors are checked to such an extent that the number of results to be recalled by future researches, will well bear comparison with the mistakes made in any other science.

To reject all the results of this method of inductive examination, because some are false, is like refusing to use any money because there are some forgeries ; or like a gold-digger throwing away all he finds, because it may be pyrites, instead of reserving it for future tests.

CHAPTER II.

APPLICATION OF THE DOCTRINE OF PROBABILITIES.

(14) BEFORE considering the question of errors in measurement, it may be well to state shortly the methods of ascertaining the probable error, and the meaning of the term, as so little attention is usually given to this subject.

Every measurement ever made, and every statement however exact, that is beyond pure geometry or mathematics, has some amount of error. The amount, however, is unknown, and all that can be done is to say that there is a certain probability of the truth not lying *beyond* a certain distance from the stated amount. Of course the probability of the truth lying within a limit, varies with the limit of error assigned; but on the average, if a sufficient number of measures or estimates of any fixed quantity be taken, it will always be found that the distribution of the errors will be about the same—*i.e.*, that if a hundred measurements are taken of the same unvarying object, and 50 of them are (say) within 1 inch of the mean of all the measures, then 82 of them will be within 2 inches of the mean, and 96 of them within 3 inches of the mean. Thus if it is known what percentage of the estimates are within a given distance of the mean, it is, therefore, known (by a table, or the curve of probabilities) what percentage are within any other given distance from the mean, or what probability there is of the truth lying within that given distance.

As with series or groups of measures, so with results from more complex data; if we know the probability of the exact truth being within a given quantity from the statement, we can also find what probability there is of the truth exceeding or being within any other given variation on the statement. The "probable error" (marked $\pm$) is the term usually applied to the extent of variation which the exact truth is as likely to lie within as beyond—*i.e.*, the distance on either side of the stated result, within which 50 per cent. and beyond which 50 per cent. of the estimates or measures will lie, if a sufficient number be taken to give a fair average. Thus 163 inches $\pm$ 4 would mean that the truth was as likely to be within the limits $163 - 4$ to $163 + 4$ (*i.e.*, 159 to 167), as beyond those limits. And as, for instance, thrice the probable error corresponds to only $\frac{1}{25}$th of the probability, therefore, in the above case, it is 25 to 1 that the truth lies between $163 - (3 \times 4)$ and $163 + (3 \times 4)$ —*i.e.*, between 151 and 175 inches.

(15) The amount of the probable error itself, being a fallible statement, has a probable error of its own. Allusion is seldom or never made to this second probable error; but it is worth consideration, practically, as showing that it is useless to state the probable error exact to hundredths (or three places of figures, as some eminent *savans* have done) when *it* has a probable error of perhaps a tenth of its whole amount—*i.e.*, is just as likely to be beyond say 9 and 11, as to be between those numbers.

Strictly speaking, every statement has an infinite series of probable errors, for the probable error of the statement itself has a probable error; and, again, this second probable error has a certain probability of error, like any other definite statement, and so on *ad infinitum*. In a few cases of the units worked as samples, the second probable error was about ⅕th of the first—*i.e.*, the amount of the first probable error was just as likely to lie beyond limits a third of its whole amount apart, as to lie within such limits; and the third, fourth, and fifth probable errors had each about the same relation to the preceding one. Probably, however, none beyond the second probable error will ever be required in any subjects.

The practical result of this fact, that the probable error has itself a considerable probable error, is that it is hopeless to try to ascertain the probable error of any statement with any great exactitude, except in the rare case of the differences of the measures from the mean being all equal. And, moreover, it is useless as well, for it can matter but little whether the probable error is rather more or less; as it is of small consequence in almost any case whether it be either 30 or 40 to 1 against or for a given supposition.

(16) There are several methods of ascertaining the amount of the probable error, but to give the simplest will suffice, and farther details may be obtained from De Morgan's Essay, or in the Cyclopædias under *Mean, Probabilities*, &c.

First, a mean of the various observations or estimates should be taken, as in ordinary averaging (unless they have varying weights), and then the difference of each estimate from the mean; these differences should be each squared, and the sum of the squares taken. Then

I. $\dfrac{\sqrt[2]{\text{sum of squares of differences}}}{\text{number of observations}} \times \cdot 674 = \text{probable error.}$

and this is the simplest form usually worked.

Now there is generally but little difference (perhaps ⅛th or so) between

II. $\dfrac{\sqrt[2]{\text{sum of squares of diffs.}}}{\text{number of observations}}$ and $\dfrac{\text{mean of differences}}{\sqrt[2]{\text{number of observations.}}}$

therefore, without introducing any error worth consideration into the result, we may say

III. $\dfrac{\text{mean of differences}}{\sqrt[2]{\text{number of observations}}} \times \tfrac{7}{10} = \text{probable error.}$

For practical use a still shorter method may be taken, which becomes worth using when many cases have to be worked. This farther abbreviation does not tend to practically increase the error of the probable error, and merely consists in using the taking of differences for the probable error, to supersede the necessity for taking an exact average to begin with. The small error that this method introduces tends to the increase of the statement of probable error; and thus to neutralise the error produced by the substitution in No. II. above, which tends, when unchecked, to slightly decrease the statement.

The reason of it will be plain enough without explanation, and the method stands thus :—Guess an average as nearly as it can be quickly done; take the differences between it and each observation, arranging them in two columns + and − according as the observation is greater or less than the guessed average. Take the sum of the + and of the − differences separately, subtract whichever is the lesser from the other, and divide the remainder by the number of observations. Add this result to the guessed mean if the + sum be greater than the − sum, and subtract if the − sum be the larger. This gives the true mean, whatever the guessed mean may have been. The two sums of the differences may now be added together, ÷ $^2\sqrt{}$ number of observations, and × $\frac{7}{10}$ to give the probable error as mentioned above.

(17) By the foregoing method, however, no notice is taken of the difference of accuracy that there may be between the observations, and, in fact, it assumes that each one is equally valuable. This is scarcely ever the case, therefore each observation must be weighted according to the square of its accuracy. If all the measurements are accurate to the same absolute quantity (say $\frac{1}{10}$ inch), then the value of each is proportionate to the square of its length. Generally, however, in using measurements it is necessary to consider how accurate each is, and to weight it accordingly. For instance, if a measure is stated to within half a foot, it has only a 6 × 6th (36th) of the weight of one stated to within an inch, allowing, of course, for any difference of length.

When the measurements differ in value very much, an unduly low result for the probable error is obtained by dividing by the square root of the whole number of observations; and the square root of the number of heavier weighted observations should be used instead.

(18) For a short, but complete, example of every step in extracting a unit, we may take the following measures of the small synagogue of Kefr Birim, from a Palestine Exploration statement :—

	Ft. In.=Ins.	Units.	Ins. per unit.	Weight.	Guessed mean 8·125. Differences weighted. +	−
Internal length .	48 6=582 ÷	72 =	8·083	100		4·2
„ breadth .	35 6 426	52½	8·114	50		·55
Wall thick . .	2 9 33	4	8·250	1	·12	
Intercolumniation	6 1 73	9	8·111	50		·7
Pedestal + base of column . .	2 8½ 32½	4	8·125	36	0	
Shaft + capital .	10 10¾ 130¾	16	8·172	150	7·05	
Diameter of shaft, mean . .	2 0½ 24½	3	8·167	10	·42	
				397	7·59	5·45

Then $7·59 - 5·45 = 2·14$

$$\frac{2·14}{397} = ·0054$$

$8·125 + ·005 = 8·130$ true mean

$7·59 + 5·45 = 13·03.$

$$\frac{13·03}{397} = ·033 \text{ mean difference.}$$

Now, as has been mentioned, if the weights differ very much, the divisor of the mean difference should be the square root of the number of those that are heavier weighted. Accordingly here $^2\sqrt{\ }4$ is probably the truest divisor, and, therefore, $(·033 \div ^2\sqrt{\ }4) \times ·7 = ·012$ probable error.

This same instance strictly worked, without any abbreviations in the method, gives $·0136 \pm ·0042$ for the probable error, so that the probable error is as likely to be beyond the limits ·009 to ·018 as between those limits. Thus it is clear that the approximate and much shorter method is perfectly good, for all purposes where secondary probable errors are not thought worth attention.

The numbers of units in each length were obtained by ratios between the measures, and though 52½ may seem an unlikely multiple, yet as the breadth is divided into

3 aisles, they will each be 17½ wide, a number not at all unusual, being ¼ of 70; also the internal length, 72 units, + end walls of 4 units each, gives 80 units for the external length. The total height of columns is 16 + 4 units, 20 in all; and the intercolumniation is 9 units, the diameters being 3, giving 12 units for distances of centres of columns. Thus all the numbers of units are likely, both in the items and in compound lengths.

The weights were assigned as already mentioned; 33 inches has little weight, because it is probably only correct to the nearest quarter of a foot. The main dimensions are only stated to the nearest half foot. The shaft and capital has less weight than it would otherwise have, because long vertical measures are always the most awkward to make, and, therefore, the less accurate.

The rest of the working is already explained in detail before (16 and 17). But it may be added that it is seldom worth while to include the least accurate measures in taking the mean; and a selection of half or two-thirds of all is the most suitable.

(19) To complete this part of the subject, the probability of the truth lying beyond given distances from the mean is appended :—

Variation in terms of probable error = unity.	Probability 1 *in*
·5	1·4
1·0 (probable error)	2·
1·5	3·2
2·0	5·7
2·5	11·
3·0	23
3·5	56
4·0	145
4·5	420
5·0	1380
5·5	4800
6·0	19200

Thus out of 23 instances, only one would have the real error of the statement more than thrice the amount stated as its probable error. And it is about 20,000 to 1 against a quantity really differing 6 times its probable error from the value stated.

The use of probable errors must be a main feature in all accurate metrology; without ascertaining the probable error of our knowledge of two units, it is impossible to know whether they are, or are not, likely to be connected. But when it is known how likely it is for a given unit to vary to any given extent, we obtain a correct idea of the likelihood of its identity with any other given unit.

Of course another element has to be included in the consideration, if our knowledge of the length of any particular unit is fairly accurate; for then the likelihood of variability of the unit in ancient times, exceeds the uncertainty of our knowledge of its length.

(20) A question in averaging that seems to have been yet unconsidered, is the weighting of a series of contiguous spaces, such as the breadths of a row of equal ornaments, or the spaces on a divided rod. There always must be small errors in the division, and the question is what value should be assigned to the length of each space in taking a mean.

If the spaces are merely produced by stepping with a compass, or some such recurrent method, the simple mean of all will be the truth—*i.e.*, the sum of the lengths divided by the number of spaces.

But, on the contrary, there is the case of a subdivided rod, and other cases of contiguous spaces, in which the dividing marks are probably copied direct from a more accurate standard; and in such cases it is evident that the intermediate marks must have *some* value as giving data of the original standard, whereas a simple mean of all the spaces, gives in reality no value to any of the marks except the two terminals.

There is more than one way of regarding this problem of the weighting of a series of approximately equal spaces. We will suppose ten spaces to be the number in question. The first method is by considering the marks as giving a collection of independent lengths, never taking the *same* mark twice over; thus taking lengths of 10 spaces (between the ultimate marks), 8 spaces (between the penultimate), 6 spaces (between the antepenult), 4 spaces, and 2 spaces; of course dividing these lengths by the number of contained spaces, to give the mean value of a space. These lengths should be weighted according to the square of their length. The second method is opposite in principle; it is to successively take every mark in the scale as a zero, and from it to take the distance to every other mark as giving a datum. Thus every mark is similarly treated by taking it as a zero in its turn, and in 10 spaces there will be 10×10 lengths taken. More properly each of these lengths should be weighted according to the square of its length.

Now it so happens that both the first and second methods, and the second method weighted as the square of the lengths, all give exactly the same result; and as both methods seem to be based on independent and rational views, we may accept their agreement as a token of their truth.

(21) The value to be assigned to each space by these methods is very simply ascertained, without going through them each time; it is *the number of the space*

counting from one end of the series × *the number counting from the other end.*

So the beginning of the series of all possible cases will stand thus: the first two cases of one and two spaces are, of course, only put in to begin the series :—

1	2	3	4	5	6	7	8	9	10	11	12
	2	4	6	8	10	12	14	16	18	20	22
		3	6	9	12	15	18	21	24	27	30
			4	8	12	16	20	24	28	32	36
				5	10	15	20	25	30	35	40
					6	12	18	24	30	36	42
						7	14	21	28	35	42
							8	16	24	32	40
								9	18	27	36
									10	20	30
										11	22
											12

Sum of weights 1 4 10 20 35 56 84 120 165 220 286 364

Thus a length divided into 5 spaces should have the first weighted 5, the second 8, the third 9, the fourth 8, and the last 5 ; in a length of 8 equal spaces they should be thus weighted : 1st 8, 2nd 14, 3rd 18, 4th 20, 5th 20, 6th 18, 7th 14, and the 8th 8. In the cases where the number of spaces is even, it is clear that the above values might be all halved before use. This method was practically used in determining the true mean length of that Egyptian cubit rod—the Harris cubit of Karnak—in the British Museum ; the results were published in *Nature,* Vol. XIV., p. 168.

It will, perhaps, appear paradoxical to say that a series of spaces should not be weighted equally. By the two different methods above, it is plain that the middle spaces have more weight ; these may be termed synthetic proofs ; but we will now take an analytic view of the question. For instance, if a space in the middle of a

D

series is rather longer than the other spaces on each side of it, it is then evident that that space separates one half of the dividing marks from the other half; it thereby should have more value in lengthening the mean unit than if the simple average of all the spaces is taken, because really the true mean is more than the simple average, owing to the greater part of the lengths being too long to be in proportion to the average. If the long space is at one end, however, it merely is long itself, and does not make the value of the unit shown by the other distances long also; thus it is evident that it should have less weight than the middle spaces. Another view is, looking at the dividing *marks* and not at the *spaces;* if a mark is misplaced near the middle of a series it matters but little,* for it shortens nearly as many distances from it on the one side as it lengthens on the other; but if a mark at one end is in error it has no compensation, and thus errors at the ends being of far more importance than errors in the middle, it is quite consistent that the end spaces should have less weight than those in the middle.

If the spaces are not of approximately equal lengths— *e.g.*, if some be intentionally double or triple the length of others, then the above values for each space × the square of the length of the space will be the weight assignable to it.

This method of weighting a series of spaces need only be used when great care is desirable, and hardly need be applied to common instances of contiguous lengths; con-

---

* The centre mark of an uneven number of marks has no value at all, for however much to one side it may be, the distances on one side of it are lengthened as much as those on the other side are shortened.

sidering how far uncertain it is whether they were all marked off from a standard at one operation, or whether they were measured cumulatively.

(22) In such a subject as metrology, where a few fresh measures may so readily modify the results to a slight extent, refinements in accuracy are not worth much care, so long as the errors overlooked do not affect the result more than a small fraction of its probable error; and the exact value of the probable error itself, so much affected by a single good or bad measure, need not be ascertained with great care (especially remembering the large extent of the secondary probable error), and we may be satisfied so long as it is correct within about a quarter of its whole amount.

The principal care should be to have the methods clearly in mind, and to observe all causes of error or modifying circumstances in each case; then allowances can be made with sufficient accuracy for occasional complex and uncertain elements (such as a chance of some apparently good measure not being really accurate), without needing to enter into applications or researches of out-of-the-way laws to work such cases; for the time occupied in such researches would often be sufficient to go and re-measure the object. In the results given in this essay, the probable error stated has been slightly modified, when necessary, to the nearest integral figure, but never beyond $\frac{1}{5}$ or perhaps $\frac{1}{4}$ of the strict amount; and it is. always stated at more rather than less than the true quantity, as it is in all cases too little rather than too much, owing to its not including the unknown errors of the measure originally used by the builders.

(23) In grouping units together which are apparently all copies or derivatives of the same, there are two ways of taking the mean unit from them all. If the units are farther from the mean than the extent of their probable errors—*i.e.*, if their probable errors do not reach the mean—then it is evident that the errors of copying them from their prototype are greater than the errors of the using of them by the builder. In such a case, as we know not which unit best represents the original, we can only take the mean of all of them ; irrespective of what may have been the errors in using them, shown by their probable error.

On the contrary, if the probable errors all overlap— *i.e.*, if one mean unit would fall within or close to the limits of probable error of each unit—then the errors of making the copies of the units originally, were less than the errors of the builders in using them and of our knowledge of them. Therefore each unit should be valued according to the accuracy with which we know its length, and thus each unit should be weighted inversely as the square of its probable error. The two methods generally give nearly the same result, usually within the extent of probable errors. Practically speaking, most of the groups of units do not agree to either of these hard and fast rules, as the probable errors of some overlap, and others stand aloof; a result between those given by the two methods above is then adopted, nearer one or the other as the case may require; this is stated as the mean in the following pages of results when no special distinction is made.

These details of the application of the theory of probable errors to the questions of metrology, are mentioned for the use of others who may wish to pursue the subject farther, and also to explain the methods used to obtain the following results. And though the preceding pages will seem familiar and elementary to the mathematician, yet antiquaries who are interested in metrology may not all have examined the subject of probable errors.

CHAPTER III.

(24) THE probable error of our knowledge of a unit is usually a compound from two sources—the original errors in planning and executing the work, and the errors made in the measurement of it in modern times; these latter may, of course, be tolerably avoided.

To discriminate whether the probable error is mainly due to the ancient or the modern errors, it should be observed whether the measurements of parts that are certain to have a given relation to each other (equal or otherwise) differ from each other more than the supposed errors of measurement. If the measures are taken on purpose to extract the unit, it is well to carefully measure the same subject in different parts, measuring it so carefully as to find some real difference between the measurements plainly beyond the extent of their likely errors; thus there is a certainty that the errors found are wholly due to the ancient errors of workmanship.

In using ordinary measures, only accurate to about a 50th of the whole amount (such as those of most travellers), the probable error may be entirely attributed to errors of measurement.

Measures of *positions* are better than absolute dimensions of stones. Weathering and wear always tend to slightly decrease the dimensions of blocks; but the dimensions of buildings, the distances of walls apart, or of marks on the faces of stones, are all practically unaltered by circumstances which affect all alike, and are, therefore, the most suitable in accurate researches.

In all measurements that I have made for the object of ascertaining the units of various remains by the inductive methods described, the errors of measurement are far less than the errors of workmanship; therefore in stating the resulting units an asterisk is placed against the probable errors (except to remains in the British Museum, all of which are given from my own measurements) to show that they are due to the errors of workmanship, and not to errors of measurement.

Though it is of little value to determine the unit from only two or three merely ordinary measures; yet from those measurements that I have made, the results may probably be rather more trusted, as in most cases each length was carefully measured twice or oftener in different parts, and the mean of the different measures taken as the true dimension.

(25) Caution is necessary in using the materials given by travellers and antiquaries; for instance, in the grand French work, " Description de l'Égypte," many of the plates are covered with measures which are worthless, though apparently very accurate; the *savans* measured sometimes in round numbers of French feet, and then reduced these rough materials to *millimètres !* A similar misleading appearance of accuracy is to be found in some other French works. Texier's and Flandin's volumes are, however, clear of this blot, but it is instructive to examine their independent measures of the same remains at Persepolis and elsewhere. Differences of a

décimètre in statements made in centimètres are quite usual; they often agree, however, within two or three centimètres. There are some curious differences, however, in the long lengths—a mètre or more in the "Salle des Trônes," for instance.

English authors also, in translating foreign measurements into English feet and inches, very often seem unconscious of the falsity of stating a result to two or three places of figures farther than in the original. These apparently correct results are very misleading, and it is worth while, if there is a suspicion of them, to glance over some of the measures on the slide rule, to see whether they are rough numbers of mètres or of French or German feet.

If this erroneous method of translation is not noticed, an innocent student of metrology might prove by inductive methods, that the early Egyptians used the French foot and mètre, and that the English foot was used at Sipylus, according to Texier's statements of the circular rough stone tombs, which seem to be merely reductions of English measures of whole feet.

Unfortunately, in the cases of the rougher monuments, such as cromlechs, &c., it is seldom that travellers favour us with any measures; still rarer is it to get accurate measures, and the rarest thing is to find a definite statement as to the working or dressing of the stones, whether they are rounded or only naturally cloven blocks, or whether they are worked into shape.

Among the many modern travellers whose works I have copied from, there are few who give good measures that will compare with Stuart and Revett, or with the better of the French expeditions, such as Texier's.

Dennis's "Etruria," Dodwell's "Cyclopean Remains," and Davis's "Carthage" are perhaps the most useful works.

(26) In examining measures of ancient buildings, especially churches, care should be taken to separate the measures belonging to work of different epochs; as there is no certainty (but rather the reverse) of the same unit having been employed for centuries together in the same place. In the subsequent additions to a building, such dimensions as are necessitated by the form of the older parts, will not be in even numbers of the unit used in the rest of the addition. A church is often built on old foundations; then the plan will, of course, give the old unit of the foundation epoch; while the doors, windows, and all the heights, will be in terms of the later unit. The buttresses on the outside of a church are always worth attention, if the inside is not examined, as their centres show the positions of the arches, and this is generally an ancient measurement, because the foundations of the pillars would be often used in rebuilding.

Another source of confusion, especially in English buildings, may arise from foreign architects, who sometimes came over to superintend the building in affiliated monasteries. Such an architect might lay out the building with his own measure, and leave the country masons to use theirs for the details.

From these considerations it seems most suitable, when some of the measures of a building agree well to a unit, and others thoroughly disagree, to examine the dissentients whether they will agree to another unit; and if so, to see whether the distribution of examples of the two units, is accountable on any of the above possibilities. If not, probably one or other, or perhaps both, of the units are fallacious.

(27) In all constructions of all dates it is most desirable, before attempting to extract the unit, to consider if any simple scheme can be traced in the form; to observe what parts are symmetrical, what may have been added to a regular plan, either when first built or later, and to see whether there is any simple proportion, 1 : 2, 1 : 3, 2 : 5, or any such ratio, between the principal dimensions; if so, to ascertain whether this ratio is true of the inside or outside, as this will give the clue as to which parts were even multiples of the unit. In a church, observe whether the tower arch be equal to the chancel arch, or the breadth of the tower equal to the nave, or what mode of dividing the nave and aisles (inside, outside, or in middle of walls), gives a simple relation between their widths. Such ideas of the original plan, show what dimensions were first set out, and what may be merely resultant, and thus not in simple numbers of units.

To obtain some idea of the design of each building is also desirable in order to know in what parts to expect simple numbers of units. For instance, inside measures may have been the guide in laying out a building, and if so, assigning such a length as 41 units $(35+3+3)$, or 37 $(32+2\frac{1}{2}+2\frac{1}{2})$ to the outside need not be objectionable, as the inner length and thickness of walls may both be simple multiples.

We may fairly expect to meet with some buildings in which the leading dimensions point out a unit, to which some of the minor features are found not to agree; there always will be buildings in which important and symmetric parts are laid out by measure, and yet some little things allowed to be made of any size that the materials or position best permitted, irrespective of attending to simple multiples of units throughout.

It will be far easier to work the subject, after having grouped the units together to form mean units, as has been done in this essay. No grouping was done until the present amount of material was collected, in order to try to avoid false grouping on insufficient data; which would prejudice the results, and be a hindrance to correct views afterwards.

(28) One of the simplest results, that may be expected from the careful examination of ancient works, is the average accuracy of workmanship in different times and countries. This is no mean test of a species of civilisation; correctness in work is one of the proofs of superiority on which mechanical men continually dilate, as showing the progress of the present age. It should be remembered, however, that Egypt in its earliest days, could turn out stone work as yet unsurpassed for its true lines and angles.

To estimate the accuracy of work we need measures of greater accuracy; therefore hardly any, except those measures made on purpose, are sufficiently accurate. The probable error does not express the accuracy of work, because the number of measures taken is a factor in it; the true expression of the accuracy is the mean of the differences between the unit deduced and the various representations of it, which is taken as an element in the probable error (16). This mean difference shows the proportion of error made on an average in the length of one unit, so stating this error in decimals of the mean unit as unity, reduces all the instances of error of workmanship to a comparable form (181).

(29) An important result that may be looked for, is the settlement of the questions of absolute or approximate ratios between ancient standards. By pure induction from the monuments, unbiassed or checked by other data, it may be hoped that the *exact* value of all ancient standards will be obtained; not merely for one place or for one time, but the mean value over countries and centuries, which will be far more reliable. Then the data will be obtained for giving full effect to Boeckh's admirable distinction.

The only way to avoid foregone conclusions, is to begin by assuming that every standard found was independent, and unconnected by simple ratios with any other standard; when correct values have been obtained for each standard, then all real connections and derivations will be manifest. Literary metrology is a heavy trammel in forming correct conclusions, if implicitly trusted; for the facility of expressing unknown standards in simple terms of known standards was, in general, too tempting to be resisted by ancient authors. To assume, for instance, that every standard used in ancient Egypt (such as those marked on the cubit rods) was formed from a simple number of digits, and that all standards were derived from digits or palms, is to fetter ourselves with an unproved conclusion; we should the rather look to the monuments to find the true units, and then see how they will agree with the other approximate information. To do otherwise, is to return to the deductive state of the subject, which was broken up by Boeckh's distinction between approximate and accurate ratios.

Between the 20·6 and 25 inch cubits, false connections of the ratio of 5 : 6 have been made by ancient authors, because they simply stated the nearest ratio; but by obtaining the accurate values of these units, it is clear that no simple connection existed between them. This is an example of the way in which approximate ratios may be foisted into the subject, to the confusion of all accuracy.

By inductive metrology giving us the more exact values of ancient standards, the argument for the connection of standards from their exact agreement will be greatly strengthened : the proof of the connection of two standards, when their lengths are uncertain within perhaps a fiftieth of the whole, cannot be of much force; but when their probable error is but a five-hundredth, the argument from their equality becomes of great value.

(30) The quantity of standards professed to be found in each country by inductive methods, may appear an objection to their correctness. This result is certainly not due to any personal bias, for these researches were begun solely to obtain accurate values for the known units of each country, with the idea that the same unit was used in all the monuments of a country (apart from foreign workmanship), and that hardly anything could be expected in Egypt except the "Karnak" cubit, or in Greece except the Olympic foot. This notion, based on preconceived ideas drawn from the literature on the subject, has gradually melted away; and the unity of the manner of the past and present use of measures, seems more and more apparent.

The number of mean units finally resulting is not at all astonishing, in fact less than might perhaps be expected, considering, as Don Quiepo says, the "infinite variety of measures." In most countries six or eight standards seem to have been in use, many of them being editions of well-known and widespread units, which travelled far on the waves of civilisation. Mediæval

England is the most extreme case of variety yet found, though perhaps other countries, if as fully examined, might equal it; and yet even this appears the pattern of simplicity and unity, when compared with the multiplicity of measures that prevailed within the present century on the Continent. Every important town of Germany, Switzerland, and Italy had its own standards; and many places were afflicted with three independent and incommensurable linear units.

To expect that countries, in most of which there was less communication than during the last few centuries on the Continent, and in many of which there was a great mixture of races and civilisations,—to expect that such countries should have but one or two standards, is against all analogy; the surprising thing is that any extent of uniformity or classification can be found, considering the small extent of the examination; and it rather seems to point to a greater care and attention bestowed on measures in the more remote ages, than during the last thousand years.

When the Continental antiquities of the Middle Ages shall have been thoroughly examined, and their units extracted, we may then hope to obtain the origin of all the units of England, and a history of every foot and ell used in recent times: they should be traced back through their imperceptible variations until the chaos of standards is reduced to order, and the prototypes, kinships, and history of each of them is defined. Thus a mass of information on the migration of tribes, and on the progress of skilled labour, will be obtained; which, in combination with our present knowledge, will throw an unsurpassed light on the history of Europe.

CHAPTER IV.

EGYPT.

(31) HAVING explained in the foregoing pages, the principles and details of the inductive examination of ancient monuments, we will now proceed with the results that have been produced, by the application of these methods to the ancient remains of different countries.

Egypt is the first land to claim attention, for the antiquity of its structures, for the effect of its civilisation on that of other lands, for the independent evidence that we have as to its units, and for the large quantity of measures that are available.

In naming the subject from which each unit is deduced, " B. M." is put for those remains which are in the British Museum (all carefully measured by myself,) and the number following is that given in the Museum ; the places from which the remains came are mentioned when known. The small number which precedes the subject of every unit, is the number of independent lengths from which the mean value of the unit was derived; where several measures are taken of the same dimension they are but counted as one. The date is given by the dynasty. The unit exactly as obtained from the measures next follows, with its probable error ; then the multiple that it presumably is of the mean unit ;

an1 finally the value for the mean unit resulting from the monument in question, and its probable error. In most cases the mean unit would fit the measures, with multiples as simple as those units first obtained from the measures; but those actually obtained are given exactly as extracted in each case, to avoid any apparent or real *cooking* of the results.

The units are all stated in British inches, and are arranged in the order of the value they give for the mean unit, that thus any connection of dates, places, or method of multiplication, with the variations in length, might be more easily seen.

(32) The first is a well-defined group of units:—

Subject.	Dynasty.	Units.	±	Multiple.	Mean unit.	±
[5]B. M. Altar . .		1·796	·003	= 4 ×	·4490	·0008
[6]B. M. 827 . .	12	·900	·002	2	·4500	·0010
[5]B. M. 63 Karnak	22	·4509	·0006	1	·4509	·0006
[2]B. M. 59*. . .	Roman.	11·305	·002	25	·4522	·0001
[2]B. M. 945 . .		4·523	·002	10	·4523	·0002
[13]Jeezeh, tomb . .	4 ?	33·96	·03	75	·4528	·0004
[6]B. M. 28 Thebes	19	1·814	·006	4	·4535	·0015
[6]Jeezeh, tomb . .	4	9·077	·017	20	·4538	·0009
[31]Jeezeh, 2nd Pyramid	4	13·63	·01	30	·4543	·0003
[8]Jeezeh, 6th Pyramid	4	13·65	·02	30	·4550	·0006
[2]B. M. 187 . .	11	5·71	·01	12½	·4564	·0008
[8]B. M. 100 . . .	11	4·577	·016	10	·4577	·0016

A fair mean of these [considering both the simple mean, and that by weighting inversely as the square of the probable error, see (23)] is ·4530 ± ·0003 inches.

(33) The following group gives the form of the 25 inch or Royal Persian cubit :—

	Dyn.	Units. $\pm$			Mean unit. $\pm$	
[10]B. M. 108 . . .	19	2·502	·006	5	·5004	·0012
[3]B. M. 70b . .	30	·5015	·0001	1	·5015	·0001
[4]B. M. 947 Siout	19	·803	·001	$\frac{8}{5}$	·5020	·0007
[2]Jeezeh tomb . .	4 ?	25·1	·1	50	·5020	·0020
[9]B. M. 527 Jeezeh	4	1·573	·004	$\frac{50}{16}$	·5034	·0012
[8]B. M. 569 . .	12	·3792	·0005	$\frac{3}{4}$	·5058	·0006

Here 1·573 is connected in a very likely way with this mean unit, as it results from a simple binary division by 16, or a continued halving, of the 25-inch cubit, of which this unit is clearly the Egyptian edition. The connection of the units ·803 and ·3792 might be considered too complex to be likely. A fair mean is ·5023 $\pm$ ·0004 : if ·803 and ·3792 were omitted, it would be ·5016$\pm$·0003. Perhaps in the uncertainty ·5020 $\pm$ ·0004 might as well be adopted. This $\times 50 = 25\cdot10\pm\cdot02$ for the cubit One unit occurs which is probably a straggler from this group, modified by some accidental circumstance ; it is

[10]Thmuis, monolith . . 25·48 $\pm$ ·01 $\div$ 50 = ·5096 $\pm$ ·0002.

(34) Another group is as follows :—

	Dyn.	Units. $\pm$			Mean unit. $\pm$	
[4]B. M. 20 . . .	20	2·6746	·0015	4	·6686	·0004
[3]B. M. Abukir .	Cent. 2	·3362	·0001	$\frac{1}{2}$	·6724	·0002
[7]B. M. 462 . . .	12	·2700	·0008	$\frac{2}{5}$	·6750	·0020
[5]B. M. 528 Jeezeh	4	3·378	·005	5	·6756	·0010
[6]B. M. 531 Jeezeh	4	3·381	·013	5	·6762	·0026
[2]B. M. 91 . . .	18	·6787	·0004	1	·6787	·0004
[2]B. M. 514 . . .	18	3·407	·003	5	·6814	·0006
[4]B. M. (King An)	12	·6846	·0003	1	·6846	·0003

The mean is ·6765 $\pm$ ·0001. There is one unit, apparently a straggler from these,

[4]B. M. 54 . . . 18 ·6971 $\pm$ ·0007.

E

(35) The next group gives the Royal Egyptian cubit :—

	Dyn.	Units.	±		Mean unit.	±
[5]Damietta monolith . .		20·42	·02	1	20·42	·02
[6]Antinoe, triumphal arch		4·088	·008	$\frac{1}{5}$	20·44	·04
[3]Siout, chambers . . .		10·24	·03	$\frac{1}{2}$	20·48	·06
[7]B. M. 113	20	·4098	·0004	$\frac{1}{50}$	20·49	·02
[11]Thebes, rock chambers .		10·25	·01	$\frac{1}{2}$	20·50	·02
[7]Antinoe, baths . . .		8·215	·012	$\frac{2}{5}$	20·54	·03
[5]B. M. 10 Alexandria .	30	2·569	·003	$\frac{1}{8}$	20·55	·03
[2]B. M. 582 (tablet) . .	12	20·57	·04	1	20·57	·04
[6]Biban el Melouk, tomb IV. West		20·58	·06	1	20·58	·06
[2]Siout, chambers . . .		20·62	·01	1	20·62	·01
[2]Jeezeh Great Pyramid*	4	41·255	·003	2	20·627	·002
[4]Bronze axe	26	2·065	·004	$\frac{1}{10}$	20·65	·04
[3]B. M. 518	18	2·066	·005	$\frac{1}{10}$	20·66	·05
[8]Jeezeh 8th Pyramid. .	4	20·66	·05	1	20·66	·05
[2]B. M. 584 (tablet) . .	12	20·67	·015	1	20·67	·015
[5]Jeezeh 5th Pyramid . .	4	20·68	·04	1	20·68	·04
[11]Jeezeh 4th Pyramid . .	4	20·70	·03	1	20·70	·03
[5]Antinoe, column of Severus		1·728	·004	$\frac{1}{12}$	20·73	·04
[6]Biban el Melouk, III. East		41·49	·08	2	20·74	·04
[13]Biban el Melouk, V. East		20·75	·10	1	20·75	·10
[10]Philae, East temple . .		3·465	·007	$\frac{1}{6}$	20·79	·04
[3]Siout, chambers . . .		12·87	·03	$\frac{5}{8}$	20·79	·05
[7]Elephantine, Nilometer divisions		20·79	·07	1	20·79	·07
[5]Antaiopolis, monolith .		8·32	·03	$\frac{2}{5}$	20·80	·08
[24]Jeezeh 3rd Pyramid . .	4	5·201	·004	$\frac{1}{4}$	20·80	·02
[3]B. M. 525 Memphis . .	30	1·665	·003	$\frac{4}{50}$	20·81	·04
[2]B. M. 42 Abydos . . .	19	2·083	·003	$\frac{1}{10}$	20·83	·03
[4]B. M. 90	Greek	1·736	·006	$\frac{1}{12}$	20·84	·07

The mean of all these is 20·64 ± ·02. This mean of these twenty-eight monumental examples is remarkably close to the mean of about a dozen examples of the cubit rods which have been discovered, as they give

* Best measures of King's chamber alone, being by far the best worked, and most concordant dimensions.

20·65 ± ·01. The oldest and most accurately worked instance of this cubit is in the King's chamber of the Great Pyramid of Jeezeh, which is 10 cubits by 20; this gives a cubit of 20·627 ± ·002, which is within the probable error of the mean from all the other monuments.

(36) The next group is distinct from the preceding, as $\frac{8}{10}$ths of an inch variation could not be attributed to a 20-inch unit; and there is a well-marked and sudden gap of $\frac{2}{10}$ inch between the groups.

	Dyn.	Units.	±		Mean unit.	±
²B. M. 168 . . .		2·100	·005	1	2·100	·005
³B. M. 111 Nitria	26	·5257	·0004	$\frac{1}{4}$	2·103	·002
²B. M. 48 Thebes	18	2·105	·004	1	2·105	·004
⁵B. M. Tablets .	Roman	3·160 ?	·012	$1\frac{1}{2}$	2·107	·008
⁵B. M. 585 tablet .	12	21·07	·015	10	2·107	·0015
²B. M. 82 . .	Roman ?	1·759	·004	$\frac{5}{6}$	2·111	·005
⁴B. M. 35 . . .	4	1·76	·01	$\frac{5}{6}$	2·112	·012
⁶B. M. 517 Karnak	22	2·118	·002	1	2·118	·002
²B. M. 74 . . .	26 ?	4·240	·003	2	2·120	·0015
⁴B. M. 83 . . .	26	·5310	·0007	$\frac{1}{4}$	2·124	·003

The mean of this compact group is 2·111 ± ·0015.

(37) The next group seems to be separate from the foregoing, as the gap between them is about twice as wide as any interval between their elements.

	Dyn.	Units.	±		Mean unit.	±
¹⁰B. M. 3 Jeezeh . . .	27	7·105	·008	$\frac{1}{3}$	21·31	·02
³B. M. 88 Karnak . .	18	2·135	·005	$\frac{1}{10}$	21·35	·05
⁵B. M. 134	26	1·604	·004	$\frac{3}{40}$	21·38	·05
⁵B. M. 133	19 ?	1·072	·001	$\frac{1}{20}$	21·42	·02
⁴B. M. 22 Alexandria .	30	5·364	·0025	$\frac{1}{4}$	21·46	·01

The mean is 21·40 ± ·02. That these units are not

mere casual coincidences, seems strongly shown by this last group having only $\frac{1}{25}$th of an inch between the examples, and yet there is no continuation of units beyond this, except one straggler :—

[2]B. M. 135* Memphis, Dyn. 25. 10·84 $\pm$ ·01, $\frac{1}{2}$ of 21·68 $\pm$ ·02.

If these units were chance numbers they would (from such a quantity) be evenly spread, and have pretty equal spaces between them; whereas, on the contrary, we find the peculiar grouping that would undoubtedly result from their being variations in the expression of one definite unit.

(38) The following is a well-defined group :—

	Dyn.	Units.	$\pm$		Mean unit.	$\pm$
[5]B. M. 60 Karnak	18	1·537	·006	1	1·537	·006
[6]B. M. (Antef) .	12	1·537	·006	1	1·537	·006
[2]B. M. 51a Thebes	18	1·157	·004	$\frac{3}{4}$	1·543	·005
[4]B. M. 476 . . .	19	1·236	·003	$\frac{4}{5}$	1·545	·004
[11]B. M. 1 and 34, Mount Barkal .	18	3·092	·002	2	1·546	·0015
[12]Karnak, Grand temple . . .		6·190	·003	4	1·547	·001
[4]B. M. 95 . . .	19	1·939	·004	$\frac{5}{4}$	1·551	·003
[8]B. M. 26 Karnak	19	1·864	·004	$\frac{6}{5}$	1·553	·004
[4]B. M. (tablets) .	12	18·74	·06	12	1·562	·005

The mean is 1·547 $\pm$ ·002. This seems like $\frac{3}{40}$ of the 20·64 group, 1·547 $\times$ $\frac{40}{3}$ = 20·63 $\pm$ ·03. The connection is so exact that this origin for it might be fairly accepted, at least until anything should contradict it. The multiples are not all pleasing; but the divisors being 5 and 4, are yet not unlikely.

(39) The following three seem to be connected :—

	Units.	±		Mean unit.	±
[8]Jeezeh, temple before 2nd Pyramid	32·84	·05	$2\frac{1}{2}$	13·14	·02
[3]B. M. 7858	·4390	·0005	$\frac{1}{80}$	13·17	·015
[6]Tanis, monolith	13·29	·04	1	13·29	·04

The mean is **13·19 ± ·02**.

Two units which are only found once are as follows :—

[4]B.M. 90. Ptolemaic or Roman . .		1·736 ± ·007
and		
[10]Jeezeh 9th Pyramid . Dyn. 4 .		9·46 ± ·01

(40) There now only remain the digits found in Egypt :—

	Dyn.	Units.	±		Mean unit.	±
[3]B. M. 777	11	2·159	·001	3	·7197	·0003
[2]B. M. 857	19	·7224	·0003	1	.7224	·0003
[4]Mehallet, monolith . .		1·445	·004	2	·7225	·0020
[10]B. M. 23	26	2·90	·01	4	·7250	·0025
[4]B. M. 800		·5814	·0002	$\frac{4}{5}$	·7267	·0003
[3]B. M. 854	19	·7283	·0006	1	·7283	·0006
[3]Siout, chambers . . .		14·58	·03	20	·7290	·0015
[3]B. M. (Pirinet) . . .	26	2·19	·02	3	·7300	·0067
[4]B. M. 62		·7304	·0006	1	·7304	·0006
[9]B. M. 469	19	·585	·002	$\frac{4}{5}$	·7312	·0025
[8]Jeezeh, sarcophagus . .	4	2·928	·002	4	·7320	·0005
[7]Jeezeh, 7th Pyramid . .	4	11·73	·013	16	·7331	·0010
[3]B. M. 70b	30	2·9365?	·0003	4	·7341?	·0001
[6]B. M. 826 Thebes . .	18	2·953	·004	4	·7382	·0010
[7]B. M. 27	19	·7386	·0006	1	·7386	·0006
[3]B. M. 512		2·225	·008	3	·7417	·0027
[2]B. M. 153 Thebes . . .	18	5·993	·002	8	·7491	·0003
[2]B. M. (16 + 52) Karnak	18	3·005	·01	4	·7512	·0025

The following diagrams will express to the eye details in the grouping of these digits, which could not be otherwise perceived. In the course of preparing this essay, every group of units in every country has been laid off in a similar way, in order to see more clearly the grouping of the units; though I have not thought it worth while to reproduce the diagrams.

The first line represents the digit magnified to five times its actual size, to make more distinct the dotted portion, which shows the extent of the variations.

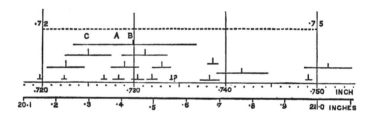

The following diagram shows the dotted portion on a scale twenty times the above size, or a hundred times the actual variations of the digit—*i.e.*, the actual variations on a length of 100 of each of the digits.

Here every unit mentioned in the above list, is represented by a short *vertical* line over its mean value on the scale below, marked from ·72 to ·75 inches; the longer *horizontal* line to each unit, showing the extent of its probable error. For instance, the digit ·7417 ± ·0027 in the list, is marked by a line over the second space from ·740—*i.e.*, over ·7417; and the horizontal line of probable error extends ·0027 on each side—*i.e.*, from ·7390 (·7417 − ·0027) to ·7444 (·7417 ± ·0027). The additional scale of 20·2 to 21·0 inches at the foot, is proportional to the digit scale of ·72, &c., inches; and shows what length any digit would be if × 28 to form the well-known Egyptian cubit of about 20·6 inches. A, B, and C are the values for the digit resulting from other measures known in Egypt, as afterwards explained in detail.

It is plain from this diagram that there are two, if not three, groups of digits, the first from ·72 to ·734 inches;* the next ·738 to ·742; and perhaps another about ·750. If these were all merely accidental varieties of one standard, they would be more evenly distributed, and it would be highly improbable that we should find such decided gaps in the spread of as many as 18 copies of the same length. The mean values of the three groups are ·7276 ± ·0010, ·7387 ± ·0002, and ·7491 ± ·0003.

The relation of the digits to the cubit scale at the foot is important. We have already seen that the cubit varied from 20·42 to 20·83; and this range of variation extends completely over the gap in the distribution of the digits (when multiplied by 28, to connect them with the cubits), and includes the whole of the ·738 group, and but a portion of the lower group.

(41) Now what may be concluded from this strange fact—remembering that we are dealing with sufficient varieties, collected from a sufficient area, to avoid any likelihood of mere accidents of distribution?

I. That the ·738 digit is thoroughly *en rapport* with the higher variants of the cubit.

II. That the ·728 group of digits are independent of the value of the cubit: if all these digits were exactly

---

* Of course the gross probable error of the ·730 digit puts its evidence quite out of the question; the conclusions must be drawn from the accurate examples.

28ths of the cubit, we should find that the group of digits and that of cubits were in exact connection; whereas the mean of the cubits is 20·64 ± ·02, and that of the digits (including all that can belong to this cubit, from ·72 to ·745) is ·73 ± ·001, which × 28 = 20·47 ±03; thus the probability against these two groups being really identical is about 650 to 1;* and the probability of the principal group (·7276) being identical with the cubit is only 1 in about five million.   Thus we may rest assured that the majority of the digits are independent of the 20·6 cubit; not a single example of that cubit appears as low as 28 × the mean value of the main group of digits; and the probability of the group of cubits and that of digits being identical is such as is not worth the least consideration.

III. That the digit and the 20·6 cubit are two incommensurable and independent units : that the original digit was usually followed when the digit was employed as a unit; and that there was a modified digit (which forms ⅙th of the examples) altered to fit the cubit, and that it is this digit consequently that is found on the divisions of the known cubit rods.

As additional evidence on this third result we may note—1st, That the number of digits, 28, is a strange one to form a cubit, and such as would alone be sufficient to raise a suspicion of independent origin.   2nd, The value given to the Egyptian cubit of 24 digits by Don Quiepo is 17·48 inches (·444 mètres), which is quite incompatible with the 28-digit cubit, ⁷⁄₆ × 17·48 being 20·39; this alone seems to show a difference in the value

---

* When two or more probable errors are combined, the resulting probable error is the ²√ of the sum of the squares.

of the digit, and 17·48 ÷ 24 = ·728 inch per digit (marked A on the diagram), which is identical with the mean value for the principal group of digits—*i.e.*, ·7276. 3rd, The mean of the various instances of a short cubit noticed by Boeckh is 18·24 ± ·01 inches; this is clearly not 24 digits, as there is no digit anywhere near the value that would result, for the digit would be ·7600, and 28 of them 21·24; clearly, then, this cannot be a 24-digit cubit. But when divided into 25 digits it gives ·7296 ± ·0005 inch per digit (marked B on diagram)— *i.e.*, just close to the most usually found short digit, which is incompatible with the 20·6 cubit. 4th, We have already found (32) in constant use a well-defined unit of ·4530 ± ·0003. This is like a 16th, or a successive halving, of ten digits; the probability against this group and the group of digits exactly coinciding in this connection being about 10 to 1: this does not put the connection beyond a fair possibility; and its simplicity and likely character are strongly in its favour. If this connection be true, it is an additional argument for the independent origin of the digit; for the mean value of the digit, from which this unit would have been derived, is ·7248 ± ·0005 (marked C in diagram), rather shorter even than the main group of digits, and therefore still farther from any connection with the cubit.

(42) It may be said that the Egyptians had started with too long a cubit to agree to their fingers; that they adhered to it as a cubit, but that they usually used their fingers for deriving digit measures, and so worked with digits that were too short in proportion to the cubit. This view assumes that they had no fixed standard for the digit measure, but merely used the fingers; we can scarcely suppose this, because they were so careful about

the cubit : also because then the digits would during many varieties of usage have varied much more than we find they do.   For instance, the four fingers taken together, and measured in precisely the same way, vary in the same hand from 2·52 to 3·10 (or ·63 to ·77 per finger,)* without going as far as the rounding of the tips or the swelling of the knuckles ; so that it would be very unlikely that we should never find a digit beyond the limits of ·72 to ·75, considering the variety of hands, and of ways of using them, apart from individual differences of fingers.   Also the fact that the mean values of the digit found in the different Mediterranean countries do not vary beyond ·720 to ·734, or a fiftieth of the whole amount, strongly shows that a permanent digit standard was in use : less variable than the fingers of Egyptians, Assyrians, Persians, Syrians, Pelasgi, Hellenes, Etrurians, and Romans, whose mean digits are all included within these limits.   Finally, if the fingers were employed we should not find such a unit derived as a 16th of 10 digits ; even if the idea of a digit was practically much connected with the fingers, they would never have divided a length of 10 fingers by successive halvings ; and this binary division was no corrupted late invention, but is found in the earliest works, and even before any known example of the digit itself.

Thus there seems no avoidance of the conclusion that the digit was an independent unit, incommensurate with the cubit ; and that it was in the earliest recorded times, established as a fixed and recognised standard of measure.

---

* Not a fancy hand of " taper fingers," but one accustomed to mechanical work.

RESULTS.

(43) The units, therefore, found in ancient Egypt are as follows, with the number of buildings, &c., in which each has been found, prefixed :—

Unit.	$\pm$	Dynasty.	Remarks.
12 of ·4530	·0003	4 to Roman.	Multiplied decimally.
			$\frac{1}{16} \times 7·248 \pm ·005$
6 of ·5020	·0004	4 to 30	Decimally treated—
			$\frac{1}{50} \times 25·10 \pm ·02$
8 of ·6765	·0010	4 to Roman.	Decimally treated.
28 of 20·64	·02	4 to Greek·	Divided decimally.
10 of 2 111	·0015	4 to Roman.	
5 of 21·40	·02	18 to 30	
9 of 1·547	·002	12 to 19	$\frac{3}{4} \times 2·063 \pm ·003$
3 of 13·19	·02		
1 of 1·736	·007	Greek or Roman.	
1 of 9·46	·01	4	
13 of ·7276	·0010	4 to 30	Treated decimally; original digit.
3 of ·7387	·0002	18 and 19	Variation of ·7276
			$\frac{1}{28} \times 20·684 \pm ·006$
2 of ·7491	·0003	18	Variation of ·7276
18·24	·01		Mean of monumental instances mentioned by Boeckh.
			$25 \times ·7296 \pm ·0005$

(44) Having thus stated the inductive results from the monuments, so far as the examination of them has yet gone, it will be well to turn to some of the other sources of information for comparisons; premising that the above results were completely obtained before any examination was made of the other ancient information, and they are, therefore, wholly unbiassed.

For Egyptian measures we have the unparalleled assistance of the principal ancient units being preserved to us, marked on some of the 20·6 cubit rods which have been discovered. There are no less than 12 independent units thus marked, 4 of which are designated as cubits; besides the well-known 20·6 on which they are given. I am indebted for the details of them to the drawings of these cubits given in Don Vasquez Quiepo's essay; they are also given by M. de Saigey. We will here note the position of the various marks on the different cubit rods : the rods are all of the 20·6 cubit length, and are divided more or less completely into 28 digits each. They are here numbered thus :—No. 1, Cubit of King Horus, 18th Dynasty; No. 2, Drovetti cubit; No. 3, Nizzoli cubit; No. 4, Sharpe cubit.

On the 5th digit in No. 4, and on the 6th in Nos. 1 and 2, we have the sign of five outspread fingers. This being marked on both 5th and 6th digits, is probably intended for 5 digits, agreeing to its sign.

On the line ending the 6th there are 5 short cross lines on Nos. 1, 2, and 4 ; and on No. 2 a special dividing line. This, therefore, can vary but little from 6 digits.

On the line ending the 8th there are 5 cross lines on No. 2, and a special dividing line; also 4 cross lines on No. 4. This shows a unit of 8 digits.

The sign of the " little span" occurs on the 9th and 10th of No. 3, on the 10th and 11th of No. 1, and- on the 11th of Nos. 2 and 4 ; also 5 cross lines on the line ending the 10th on No. 1. Thus 10 digits is the only length to which all these marks can refer.

On the end of the 11th digit on No. 2 a special dividing line occurs, showing some unit of about 11 digits.

The sign of the " great span" occurs on the 12th and

13th of No. 1, on the 13th and 14th of Nos. 2, 3, and 4;
it may therefore apply to any part of the 13th digit; but
a special dividing line on No. 2, at the end of the 13th,
seems to show that it is close to 13 digits.

On the 15th of Nos. 2 and 4 there is the arm denot-
ing a cubit; and *across* the line ending the 15th on
Nos. 1 and 3 the arm holding an axe, or sceptre, (?) is
placed. This, therefore, shows a cubit of 15 digits, or
rather less.

Across the line ending the 17th of No. 3, and that
ending the 18th of No. 1, the cubit sign is placed. This
shows that this cubit is somewhere in the 17th digit,
probably about 17½.

On the line ending the 19th there are 3 cross lines
placed on Nos. 2 and 4, showing a unit close to 19
digits.

On the 22nd and 23rd of Nos. 1 and 2 the sign of the
little cubit is given, and also on the 23rd and 24th of
No. 4. This shows it to be somewhere in the 23rd digit.

On the line ending the 24th of No. 3 there is a
special dividing line; and on No. 1 also a cubit is given
of 24 digits.

On the line ending the 26th of No. 4 there are two
cross lines, showing a unit of about 26 digits.

The end of the cubit notified as the "Royal cubit"
is at 28 digits.

(45) Now these cubits and other units, nearly all
belong to the units inductively found, as the following
summary shows :—

On the cubit rods.			Units inductively found.
Sign.	Digits.	Inches.	
5 fingers . . .	5	= 3·7	
Cross lines . .	6	4·4	4·530 ± ·003, also as ·4530 ± ·003
„ „ . .	8	5·9	(5·821 ± ·008 ÷ 8=)·7276 ± ·001
Little span . .	10	7·4	(7·248 ± ·005 ÷ 16=)·4530 ± ·003
Dividing line .	11	8·1	(8·032 ± ·006 ÷ 16=)·5020 ± ·0004
Great span . .	13	9·6	9·46 ± ·01 (see 26 digits)
	(or less)	(or less)	
Cubit	15	11·0	(10·824 ± ·016 ÷ 16=) ·6765 ± ·001
	(or less)	(or less)	
Cubit	17½	12·9	13·19 ± ·02
	(about)	(about)	
Cross lines . .	19	14·0	(13·89 ± ·06 ÷ 8=) 1·736 ± ·007
Cubit	22½	16·6	(16·888 ± ·012 ÷ 8=) 2·111 ± ·0015
	(about)	(about)	
Cubit	24	17·6	
Cross lines . .	26	19·2	(18·92 ± ·02 ÷ 2=) 9·46 ± ·01
Royal cubit . .	28	20·6	20·64 ± ·02

Thus three units (4·53, 9·46, and 13·19) are marked on the cubit rods exactly as inductively found, and six others (5·821, 7·248, 8·032, 10·82, 13·89, and 16·89), being short units, are marked as multiples by 8 or 16 for the convenience of representation; this method of marking is the most likely form in which we should expect them, as by simple repeated halving the small unit would be accurately produced. To mark such units as ·502, ·676, &c., their unmultiplied length on the cubit rods, would have been of no use for practical purposes.

By induction, therefore, we obtain the exact values of the units approximately shown us on the ancient measuring rods. For seven of these—(*i.e.*, 11 digits, 13 or less, 15 or less, about 17½, 19, about 22½, and 26), there could be no reasonable supposition of an origin from the digit; and as to the others, 6 digits may belong to the digit, but the marking of this 6-digit length looks very much like a sign for the ·4530 unit, which is probably derived from the digit, and should be given as 6¼ digits. The 5-digit length doubtless refers to the simple 5 digits. But the 10-digit length may represent the 16 units of ·4530 (derived from it), just as other marks show 16 units each. The 8-digit length is the normal representation of the digit, similar to the other multiples by 8 and 16. The 24-digit length has not been yet found inductively from the monuments: this cannot be the "little cubit," as has been often supposed, because though one of the "little cubit" signs occurs on the 23rd and 24th digits, yet on *two* of the rods these signs are on the 22nd and 23rd digits, showing unmistakably that the little cubit is in the 23rd digit—*i.e.*, about 22½ digits.

It is specially worth notice that there are no marks at the half or quarters of the whole length of 28 digits, though a dozen other units are notified. This points to the digit as being the more important standard, its decimal multiple being marked; and it corroborates the conclusion that the digit and 20·6 cubit were independent; if they had not been so, the digits forming integral parts of the cubit would certainly have been noted; but the cubit being decimally divided, as is seen in the list of examples of it, the 28 digits had so little connection with the decimal scale that they were apparently regarded as having nothing to do with each other.

Thus ten of the eleven independent standards of measures, found inductively from the Egyptian monuments, are represented, on the cubit rods, or simply connected with those so shown: affording a very strong confirmation of the results in this case, where they can be tested by contemporary evidence.

(46) The sceptres borne by officials on the early

Egyptian tombs are worth notice. The usual length of the thin part is 6½ squares of the canon of proportion, and the thick end 1½ squares more. There being 19 squares to the height of a man, this gives the length of the thin part as about 23 inches, and the total 28½. This seems as if the lengths of these rods might be 32 and 40 digits (23·3 and 29·1 inches) ; and what supports the idea of such multiples of the digit, is the probability (from various sources) that the digit is a binary fraction of an original unit, as we find 8 digits marked on the cubit rods, and 16 and 32 digits formed Pelasgic and Etrurian units. The form of a thin length agreeing to one unit, and a thicker addition making the total give another unit, is found in the Edfou Nilometer.

CHAPTER V.

BABYLONIA, ASSYRIA, PERSIA, AND SYRIA.

BABYLONIA AND ASSYRIA.

(47) THESE countries are classed together, as being so intermixed in the style of their art and the nature of their remains. The dates are given in years B.C., marked with the minus sign. The digits and their multiples are found as follows :—

	Unit.	±	Multiple.	Mean unit.	±
[3]B. M. Bir, early	·72 ?	·01	1	·72	·01
[3]B. M. Nimroud, lions . .	7·24	·01	10	·724	·001
[7]B. M. cylinder seals . . .	·4835	·001	$\frac{2}{3}$	·7252	·0015
[3]B. M. Nimroud altar −880	·7298	·0004	1	·7298	·0004
[3]B. M. Kurkh Asshur-nazir-pal −880	14·65	·04	20	·7325	·002
[4]B. M. Nimroud Bulls . .	12·33	·03	$\frac{100}{6}$	·7398	·0018
[3]B. M. Nimroud Pavement.	3·70 ?	·02	5	·740	·004

The mean is ·7300 ± ·0005. This seems to be pre-eminently the Nimroud measure.

(48) The following are examples of the well-known "Karnak" cubit :—

F

	Unit.	±	Mul-tiple.	Mean unit.	±
[12]B. M. Brass bowls . . .	1·527	·005	$\frac{3}{40}$	20·36	·07
[9]Khorsabad	20·49	·05	1	20·49	·05
[21]Khorsabad.	20·51	·04	1	20·51	·04
[9]Khorsabad. Basalt temple .	1·710	·005	$\frac{1}{12}$	20·52	·06
[5]Khorsabad	4·120	·004	$\frac{1}{5}$	20·60	·02
[2]B. M. Babylonia. Seal of Dungi − 2200	2·064	·002	$\frac{1}{10}$	20·64	·02
[1]B. M. Nimroud. Nebo. −800	20·8 ?	·3	1	20·8	·3

The mean is 20·60 ± ·01, and the earliest example 20·64 ± ·02. This is apparently *the* unit of Khorsabad. Here we see the $\frac{3}{40}$ths of the cubit that we noticed as a unit in Egypt.

(49) Another cubit occurs in the following :—

		±			±
[8]Abu Shahrein, early . .	19·85	·05	1	19·85	·05
[5]Mugheyr, temple, − 1800 .	39·75	·05	2	19·87	·03
[3]B. M. Basalt monolith, early	4·024	·012	$\frac{1}{5}$	20·12	·06
[6]B. M. Kalah Sherghat . .	10·07	·03	$\frac{1}{2}$	20·14	·06

The mean is 19·97 ± ·04; this seems to be an early unit, and the grouping looks as if there were a higher and a lower variant of it.

(50) The Royal Persian cubit is found in four instances :—

		±			±
[5]Khorsabad Esarhaddon's palace	24·85	·1	1	24·85	·1
[2]B. M. Kurkh, Shalmaneser, −850	8·40	·02	$\frac{1}{3}$	25·20	·06
[6]Wurka, Wuswus	25·33	·07	1	25·33	·07
[4]B. M. Nimroud Bull por-tals with winged figures .	25·37	·04	1	25·37	·04

The mean is 25·28 ± ·04.

(51) Another unit appears in three cases :—

		±		±	
³B. M. Tablet of Vulnirari I. −1300	1·188	·002	1 ·	1·188	·002
³B. M. 101. Pavement . .	1·190?	·005	1	1·190	·005
³B. M. 2. Nimroud, −880 .	14·20	·04	12	1·192	·003

These seem to belong together; their mean is 1·189 ± ·001.

(52) These groups comprise all the units yet found inductively from Assyrian monuments. Dr. Oppert, examining the Assyrian metrology from literary remains (the Senkereh tablet, &c.), comes to the conclusion that besides the main series of Assyrian measures (the cubit of which is, according to him, 21·60 inches) there were two other units, clearly not forming part of the regular system; these he values at 25·20 inches and 39·96 inches. The Babylonian cubit he states as 20·68 inches. Now comparing these, we have the Assyrian units :—

According to Dr. Oppert.	Inductively from the monuments.
Babylonian cubit . . . 20·68	20·60 ± ·01 (earliest 20·64 ± ·02)
Assyrian cubit . . . 21·60	21·37 ± ·15 (through the 19·97, see below)
Royal cubit . . . . 25·20	25·28 ± ·04
Great U. . . . . . 39·96	39·94 ± ·08, double of 19·97 ± ·04

These inductive results were exactly determined as here stated, before Dr. Oppert's figures were examined or reduced to inches, so that they are totally independent.

The cubit of 21·37 is recovered from the monuments inductively by the following means :—In Sennacherib's inscription, Bellino's cylinder, there are several dimensions of buildings restored, given in terms of the *suklu*

rabtu, or great suklu. This we have already found to be
39·94 inches, the ʊ being the same as the *suklu*. Now
these dimensions are not simple numbers of *suklu rabtu;*
and therefore they are presumably simple numbers of
some other unit. Just as from measurements in inches
or mètres we can find the ancient unit of a building inductively, as we have been showing in the foregoing
pages; so from measures in the *suklu* we can find the
ancient unit inductively in terms of the *suklu.*

Now, inductively examining these numbers of *suklu*,
we find that they stand to each other in the ratio of the
numbers placed opposite to them below :—

Lengths, in *suklu rabtu.*		Multiple.		Unit in terms of *suklu* = 1.
134	÷	12½	=	10·72
95		9		10·55
354		33		10·73
279		26		10·73
162		15		10·80
217		20		10·85
386		36		10·72
1700		160		10·63

These multiples thus found are most of them likely
numbers, and at all events far more likely to have been
used than the very irregular numbers of *suklu rabtu.*
The mean value of the new unit is 10·70 ± ·02 *suklu
rabtu.** This great suklu or ʊ being 39·94 ± ·08 inches,
this new unit is 427·4 ± 1·1 inches. Now this
÷ 20 = 21·37 ± ·06, which is clearly the principal
Assyrian unit given by Dr. Oppert as 21·6. This 21·4

---

* This had been determined thus far, without knowing what the
suklu rabtu was (as it is merely translated "measure" in "Records
of the Past"), and, therefore, independently of any bias; and it
was only on reading Dr. Oppert's paper on Assyrian measures, and
receiving the name of the measure (kindly furnished by Prof.
Sayce), that the farther steps of reduction to English inches could
be taken.

cubit, therefore, was used by the ancient artificers whose work Sennacherib restored; or possibly the restored parts were reported in simple numbers of the 21·4 unit, and transcribed into numbers of the *suklu rabtu* by the scribe who prepared the tablet. The first two lengths mentioned on the tablet are 360 and 80 *suklu rabtu*, but these may as easily be the simple numbers of 33⅓ and 7½ of the long unit of 20 × 21·4; or 666⅔, and 150 of the 21·4 unit.

This new determination of the unit at 21·37 inches, might be perhaps accepted instead of Dr. Oppert's result of 21·60 (from the recorded circuit of an extant building), as it agrees far closer with the unit of 21·40 in Egypt, and 21·37 in Persia.

RESULTS.

The mean values of the Assyrian and Babylonian units, therefore, are as follows, with the number of buildings prefixed:—

		±	
7 of	·7300	·0005	early to − 500. Decimally multiplied.
6 of	20·60	·01	− 2200 to − 880. Decimally divided.
4 of	19·97	·04	Early.
4 of	25·28	·04	− 850, &c.
3 of	1·188	·002	− 1300 to − 800.
	21·37	·06	

PERSIA.

(53) The numbers of the Persepolitan palaces are those affixed to them by Flandin and Coste.

The following is the most usual unit :—

	Unit.	±		Mean unit.	±
[6]Persepolis IV.	12·56	·02÷	12½ =	1·005	·002
[8]Mt. Elwand, tablet . . .	3·025	·009	3	1·008	·003
[5]Shahpoor	30·24	·06	30	1·008	·002
[17]Zohab	8·083	·025	8	1·010	·003
[13]Persepolis, portal . . .	16·84	·03	$\frac{100}{6}$	1·010	·002
[17]Persepolis VI.	6·070	·006	6	1·012	·001
[7]Persepolis III.	20·27?	·03	20	1·013	·002
[7]Persepolis VIII.	20·28	·024	20	1·014	·001
[6]Pasargadæ, altar and steps	12·68	·02	12½	1·014	·0015
[3]Persepolis VII.	101·57	·06	100	1·0157	·0006
[7]Zohab	16·29	·01	16	1·0180	·0006
[8]Firouzabad, Sassanian . .	13·57	·01	$\frac{40}{3}$	1·018	·001
[4]Kala i Khuna . · . . .	25·53	·04	25	1·021	·002

The mean of these is $1\cdot013 \pm \cdot001$; this is clearly a 25th of the Royal Persian cubit, and multiples by 12½, 25, and 100 occur above. Multiplying it by 25 we have $25\cdot34 \pm \cdot02$ for the cubit; thus divided very similarly to the Egyptian 25·10, ÷ 50. The $\frac{100}{6}$ and $\frac{40}{3}$ multiples above are not unlikely, considering the neighbourhood of sexagesimal Babylonia. The following *may* be stragglers from this group :—

		±			±
[8]Fessa	994·	2·	1000	·994	·002
[10]Istakhr	12·47?	·05	12½	·998 ?	·004
[5]Ctesiphon, Sassanian . .	25·82	·03	25	1·033	·001

(54) The Egypto-Babylonian cubit is found in four cases :—

		±			±
[6]Pasargadæ	4·113	·014	⅕	20·56	·07
[17]Naksh i Roustam, Harem of Djemshid	12·40	·03	⅗	20·67	·06
[9]Istakhr	20·8	·1	1	20·8	·1
[4]Ispahan, Sassanian . . .	2·088	·012	$\frac{1}{10}$	20·88	·12

The mean is 20·70 ± ·04, and the division is clearly decimal. The 12·40 is like the Babylonian foot of $\frac{3}{5}$ of the cubit.

(55) The following five give a derived unit:—

		±			±
[8]Bi Soutoun, Sassanian . .	1·72	·01	1	1·72	·01
[21]Persepolis II.	68·86	·08	40	1·721	·002
[7]Pasargadæ	6·920	·014	4	1·730	·004
[3]Pasargadæ, Cyrus' tomb .	1·735	·001	1	1·735	·001
[5]Takht i Ghero	17·37	·03	10	1·737	·003

The mean is 1·730 ± ·002. As used in the tomb of Cyrus this unit is undoubtedly × 24. Accepting this as indicating the relationship of this unit, we may say 1·730±·002 × 24 = 41·52±·05; this is twice 20·76 ± 02 —*i.e.*, the unit is a 12th of the well-known 20·6 or ·7 cubit, and the cubit value by it agrees with that directly found from the Persian remains (20·70 ± ·04) within the limits of probable error.

(56) Another unit occurs in the following:—

		±			±
[2]Selmas	13·967	·007	$\frac{5}{6}$	16·76	·01
[5]Darabgerd	419·7	1·6	25	16·79	·06
[7]Fire altars	42·13	·16	$2\frac{1}{2}$	16·85	·06
[7]Pasargadæ, fire altars . .	28·1	·1	$\frac{5}{3}$	16·86	·06
[11]Naksh i Roustam, tomb .	10·58	·01	$\frac{5}{8}$	16·93	·02
[12]Naksh i Roustam, tomb .	8·504	·012	$\frac{1}{2}$	17·01	·024

The mean is 16·88 ± ·03. The 10·58÷$\frac{5}{8}$ seems the least likely element, but this is tolerably guaranteed by the adjoining Naksh i Roustam 8·504 being so closely as 4 : 5 to it. The $\frac{5}{6}$ and $\frac{5}{3}$ support each other, and the $\frac{5}{3}$ is also supported by the other fire altars (*Pyrées*) giving so closely the same value for the mean unit. The following may be stragglers from this group:—

	$\overset{+}{}$			$\overset{+}{}$
[2]Naksh i Roustam . . .	32·72 ·08	2	16·36 ·04
[6]Naksh i Roustam . . .	32·98 ·06	2	16·49 ·03
[7]Tak i Bostan	16·60 ·025	1	16·60 ·025

This unit is similar to the 16·888 ± ·012 unit found in Egypt on the cubit rods and from the monuments.

(57) The following are the digits found :—

	$\overset{+}{}$			$\overset{+}{}$
[8]Pasargadæ fortress . . .	14·620 ·014	2	7·310 ·007
[3]Firouzabad.	183· 1·	25	7·310 ·05
[6]Pasargadæ	73·47 ·04	10	7·347 ·004
[4]Istakhr	7·38 ·02	1	7·38 ·02

The mean is 7·339 ± ·007 for the 10 digits length.

(58) The next is a group of five units :—

	$\overset{+}{}$			$\overset{+}{}$
[6]Kengovar	3·787 ·008	5	·7574 ·0016
[10]Naksh i Roustam . . .	7·650 ·012	10	·7650 ·0012
[7]Sarbistan . . . . · ·	11·50 ·01	15	·7666 ·0008
[11]Persepolis . . . . · ·	9·59 ·03	12½	·7672 ·0025
[12]Persepolis . . . . · ·	9·6$_{06}$ ·01	12½	·7685 ·0012

The mean is ·7652 ± ·0008. This is just a 50th of a modern Persian measure, ·7652 × 50 being 38·26 ± ·04, and the Persian *arish* is 38·27 ; whether this *arish* can be clearly traced to any different source I do not know, the resemblance is at least striking, and the quinary multiples of this unit found, 5, 12½, 15, &c., bear out a multiplication by 50.

(59) The only other Persian unit is as follows :—

	$\overset{+}{}$			$\overset{+}{}$
[2]Darabgerd	71·1 ·4	$\frac{1}{8}$	21·33 ·12
[23]Persepolis platform . . .	35·58 ·06	$\frac{1}{6}$	21·35 ·04
[5]Firouzabad	42·7 ·2	2	21·35 ·1
[5]Van	42·72 ·16	2	21·36 ·08
[10]Persepolis platform . . .	53·50 ·11	2½	21·40 ·04
[5]Shiraz	2·685 ·012	$\frac{1}{8}$	21·48 ·1

The mean is 21·375 ± ·01 ; and it seems to be ÷ 3 or 6 to judge by the ⅓ and ⅙. This unit is apparently the same as the Assyrian 21·4 cubit, which was ÷3 and 60, and which Dr. Oppert has applied with slight variation to Persian buildings.*

It will be observed that the platform of Persepolis is put in twice in the list; this was due to accidentally taking Flandin's and Texier's measures separately; the units evolved from them are, however, very closely as 2 : 3—in fact, far within the probable errors. This is a good proof of the genuineness of the results, that two units so closely related should appear from two sets of different measures of the same object.

RESULTS.

(60) The following, then, are the Persian units found inductively, and the number of remains in which each has been yet found :—

13 of	1·013	·001	× 25 = 25·34 ± ·02.	Royal Persian cubit.
4 of	20·70	·04	decimally divided.	Egyptian and Babylonian cubit.
5 of	1·730	·002	decimally multiplied.	× 12 = 20·76 ± ·02.
6 of	16·88	·03	duodecimally divided.	16·88 Egyptian cubit.
4 of	7·339	·007	decimally multiplied.	10 digits.
5 of	·7652	·0008	quinarily multiplied.	$\frac{1}{50}$ of modern *arish*.
6 of	21·375	·01	duodecimally divided.	Assyrian and Egyptian 21·40.

SYRIA.

(61) This is so wide a field, including Egyptian, Babylonian, Greek, and Roman, besides its native elements, that a strict grouping is hardly suitable except

---

* The reasons why I have not accepted the details of his application of this unit to Persian buildings I have already mentioned in (8) Methods of Inductive Examination.

where the remains are clearly of the same epoch and origin. The places mentioned are in Palestine, except where otherwise stated.

The digits found are as follows :—

	Unit.	±		Mean unit.	±
[4]Medeba, &c., Moab . . .	14·42	·08	20	·721	·004
[7]Irbid, synagogue . . .	3·609	·005	5	·722	·001
[10]Zekweh temple	14·50	·02	20	·725	·001
[7]Burkush temple	5·461	·006	2·0/4	·728	·001
[10]B. M. Idalion, Cyprus . .	·733	·001	1	·733	·001
[13]B. M. Sidon, sarcophagus .	·7354	·0012	1	·7354	·0012
[9]B. M. Gebel Hauran, door	1·480	·003	2	·7400	·0015
[2]Jerusalem, sarcophagus .	·740	·003	1	·740	·003

It is useless to take a mean of elements from such different sources. The two Syrian temples give a mean of ·727 ± ·001; and the Idalion tablet and Sidon sarcophagus, which may, perhaps, be placed together, give ·734 ± ·001. See (106) on the Bashan digit.

(62) Another unit is found in the following close and well-defined group :—

		±			±
[3]Um el Amud, synagogue .	6·60	·01	2	3·300	·005
[5]Rukleh, temple	33·01	·06	10	3·301	·006
[7]Tel Hum, synagogue . .	3·304	·008	1	3·304	·008
[5]Keraseh, synagogue . . .	3·306	·006	1	3·306	·006
[6]Mashita, Moab. A.D. 620 .	13·23	·01	4	3·307	·003

The mean is 3·305 ± ·001.

(63) This group seems to be distinct from the preceding.

		±
[14]Ain Hershah, temple . . .	3·331	·005
[6]Meiron, synagogue	3·337	·007

Mean 3·333 ± ·001. These two groups (62 and 63) are probably identical in origin, but seem to be two quite

distinct varieties of the unit. For a mean we may take
3·315 ± ·007 : this × 4 (as in Mashita) = 13·26 ± ·03,
which seems identical with the Egypto-Asian unit, which
varies from 13·19 to 13·36.

(64) Another unit is shown in five instances :—

		±			±
[9]Kefr Birim large synagogue	4·031	·006	1	4·031	·006
[12]Husn Niha temple . . .	20·20	·02	5	4·040	·004
[2]El Jish synagogue . . .	4·06	·03	1	4·06	·03
[8]Burkush	6·50	·01	$\frac{8}{5}$	4·062	·007
[8]Kefr Birim small synagogue	8·13	·02	2	4·065	·005

Mean 4·049 ± ·005: this × 5 (as at Husn Niha) is
20·24 ± ·03, which may be the unit 19·97 ± ·04 of
Assyria and Asia Minor.

(65) The following group gives a well-known
cubit :—

		±			±
[5]Chambers, in Haram wall, Jerusalem	3·738	·005	$\frac{3}{20}$	24·92	·03
[6]Tomb, near Convent of Cross, Jerusalem . . .	8·32	·02	$\frac{1}{3}$	24·96	·06
[3]Gennath Gate, Jerusalem .	25·37	·1	1	25·37	·1
[8]Kulat esh Shukif, castle .	5·110	·001	$\frac{1}{5}$	25·550	·005

The mean is 25·2 ± ·1. This is the sacred Hebrew
cubit, and if we take the Jerusalem examples alone, the
mean is 25·00 ± ·03. The two following may be stragglers from this group, but we can hardly suppose a
variation of over half an inch in a unit of 25 inches :—

		±			±
[4]Arny temple	2·457	·001	$\frac{1}{10}$	24·57	·01
[8]Jerusalem, cist	6·189	·004	$\frac{1}{4}$	24·68	·02

The mean of all the six examples is 25·03 ± 3, but it is improbable that the last two should be included.

(66) The next three seem to group together :—

		±			±
[8]Fukrah temple	8·834	·025	8	1·104	·003
[4]Amâry	5·56	·02	5	1·112	·004
[4]Nakleh	14·02	·03	12½	1·122	·002

Their mean is 1·113 ± ·003 : this is probably $\frac{1}{10}$ of the Phœnician 11·1 foot.

(67) Two others are probably connected :—

		±			±
[8]Jerusalem aqueduct . .	4·27 ?	·02	3	1·423	·007
[7]Niha temple	5·714	·008	4	1·428	·002

Mean 1·427 ± ·001 : this × 4 is = 5·708 ± ·004, which may be connected with the 5·658 ± ·005 unit of Asia Minor.

(68) The Roman foot and cubit appear in the following :—

		±			±
[8]Deir el Ashayir, temple .	11·666	·007	1	11·666	·007
[16]Baalbek temple, 2nd cent..	17·50	·04	1½	11·666	·027

(69) One example of the Egypto-Babylonian cubit occurs :—

[3]Amâry tank . . . . 20·73 ± ·02.

These include all the units deduced from Syrian remains.

RESULTS.

(70) Thus we have the following units, found in the number of buildings prefixed :—

8 of	·721 ± ·004	to ·740 ± ·003. Digit.
8 of	3·315 ·007	× 4 = 13·26; 13·19 in Egypt, Asia Minor, &c.
5 of	4·049 ·005	× 5 = 20·24; 19·97 in Assyria, Asia Minor, &c.
4 of	25·2 ·1	25·28 Assyria, Persia, &c. Sacred cubit.
3 of	1·113 ·003	$\frac{1}{10}$ of the Phœnician foot.
2 of	1·427 ·001	× 4 = 5·708; 5·658 in Asia Minor.
2 of	11·67 ·01	Roman foot.
1 of	20·73 ·02	Egypto-Babylonian cubit.

Of these ·73, 25·2, 11·67, and 20·73 are well known historically, and the rest seem to be connected with units found elsewhere.

CHAPTER VI.

ASIA MINOR AND GREECE.

Asia Minor.

(71) This geographical division of land has received such a great variety of inhabitants and of civilisations, that simplicity is hardly to be looked for in its metrology. Egyptians civilised the south coast; Assyrians overran a large part; Persians conquered the whole; the Ægean coast was always more akin to Greece than to the eastern parts of the peninsula; Northern barbarians invaded its centre; and Romans conquered the whole country; to its subsequent masters we have not here to refer.

We will first notice the old 20·6 cubit.

	Unit.	±		Mean unit.	±
[5]Patara temple.	5·100	·006	$\frac{1}{4}$	20·400	·024
[5]Laodikeia temple	20·44	·06	1	20·44	·06
[9]Antiphellos, Lycian tomb .	2·054	·003	$\frac{1}{10}$	20·54	·03
[6]Ephesos, Temple of Artemis	20·552	·008	1	20·552	·008
[13]Pergamon amphitheatre .	20·57	·06	1	20·57	·06
[6]Carpuseli tomb	1·651	·005	$\frac{8}{100}$	20·64	·06
[12]Ani (Armenia) church . .	6·463	·007	$\frac{5}{16}$	20·682	·022
[6]Dighour (Armenia) church	10·384	·006	$\frac{1}{2}$	20·768	·012
[7]Ani (Armenia) cathedral .	12·992	·016	$\frac{5}{8}$	20·787	·025
[4]Aperlai theatre	20·787	·016	1	20·787	·016
[7]Mura, Roman tomb . . .	10·43	·02	$\frac{1}{2}$	20·86	·04

The mean of all these is 20·64 ± ·02. The Armenian, however, may perhaps be separated, though, as they are all Byzantine churches, Greek civilisation and work may be expected among them; they agree closely, their mean being 20·75 ± ·02, which is like the Persian variety of the cubit. The mean of the other examples, omitting Armenia, is 20·60 ± ·03. Herodotus expressly states that the Samian was the same as the Egyptian cubit.

(72) The following group is apparently derived from 20·6 :—

		$\pm$			$\pm$
[2]Sigeion	34·4 ?	·1	2	17·20	·05
[7]Phellos, monolith tomb .	2·5826	·0004	$\frac{3}{20}$	17·217	·003
[3]Pteria, city gate	17·23	·01	1	17·23	·01
[4]Mura, Corinthian tomb .	6·914	·006	$\frac{2}{5}$	17·28	·02
[11]Patara, theatre	12·98	·02	$\frac{3}{4}$	17·31	·03
[8]Antiphellos, monolith . .	·8673	·0024	$\frac{1}{20}$	17·35	·05
[17]Pteria, temple.	17·36	·01	1	17·36	·01
[3]Pteria, Akropolis . . .	17·46	·08	1	17·46	·08

The mean is 17·25 ± ·02. In Persia we have already seen the 20·7 cubit divided into 12 parts as a unit; here we have as a unit 10 of these 12ths, for 17·25 × $\frac{12}{10}$ = 20·70 ± ·02, which varies but little from 20·64 ± ·02 as found in Asia Minor, the difference being only half as much again as the probable errors. In Persia we have seen that the mean value is 20·70, and the rather high result from 17·25 may suggest that it was derived from the duodecimal division used by the Persians, and thus carried into Asia Minor.

(73) The following group shows the digit used :—

		±			±
[6]Trapezous, church, St. Sophia	14·63	·05	20	·7315	·0025
[6]Dana, Kommagene, church	24·39	·05	$1\frac{00}{3}$	·7317	·0015
[10]Nikaia, Yeni Cheher gate .	21·97	·04	30	·7323	·0013
[8]B. M. Sigeion, pedestal or altar ?		·8806	·001	$\frac{6}{5}$	·7338 · ·0008
[7]Nakoleia, Greek tombs .	7·36	·03	10	·7360	·0030

The mean is ·7330 ± ·0004, in close accordance with the digit of other countries, especially Persia.

(74) Another unit occurs as follows :—

		±			±
[4]Knidos, building. . . .	33·74	·08	6	5·623	·013
[13]Aizanoi Temple of Zeus .	22·56	·03	4	5·640	·007
[8]Iassos, theatre	8·488	·006	$1\frac{1}{2}$	5·659	·004
[8]Knidos, platform . . .	34·04	·02	6	5·673	·003
[5]Aphrodisias, Temple of Aphrodite	17·15	·02	3	5·683	·007

The mean is 5·658 ± ·005; a unit apparently found in Syria and Greece.

(75) The next may belong to the preceding :—

		±			±
[6]Ephesos, temple, 1st cent. A.D.	15·61	·03	$\frac{12}{100}$	1·873	·003
[7]Koos, cistern	9·382	·013	5	1·876	·003
[10]Mura, tomb of Arsakes .	7·52	·02	4	1·880	·005
[3]Prousa, church, St. Elias .	25·11	·03	$\frac{3}{40}$	1·883	·002
[9]Telmissos, Lycian tomb .	3·768	·002	2	1·884	·001
[2]Nakoleia, Phrygian tombs	12·6 ?	·1	$\frac{3}{20}$	1·890 ?	·015
[6]Iassos, tomb	18·92	·06	10	1·892	·006
[7]Mura, rock tomb	15·205	·03	8	1·901	·004

The mean is 1·884 ± ·001. This group seems to be very probably connected with the preceding; as 5·658 ± ·005 ÷ 3 is 1·886 ± ·002. Thus the two groups may be considered as one, with a mean of 1·885 ± ·001, which was in many cases apparently × 3, and then used as a unit.

(76) Another unit is found in nine instances:—

		$\pm$			$\pm$
[13]Nikaia, fortification, 4th cent.? A.D.	10·80	·02	1	10·80	·02
[5]Antiphellos, tomb of Ptolemaios	2·1742	·0006	$\frac{1}{5}$	10·871	·003
[6]Sipulos Akropolis . . .	13·062	·013	$\frac{6}{5}$	10·885	·01
[6]Sophon bridge, 530? A.D.	9·079	·006	$\frac{5}{6}$	10·895	·005
[6]Aperlai, baths	5·457	·003	$\frac{1}{2}$	10·914	·006
[10]Telmissos, theatre . . .	13·098	·012	$\frac{6}{5}$	10·915	·01
[3]Ludia, tomb of Aluattes .	10·95	·01	1	10·95	·01
[3]Sophon, near bridge . .	9·132	·006	$\frac{5}{6}$	10·958	·005
[7]Sophon, addition to bridge	9·238	·008	$\frac{5}{6}$	11·086	·007

The mean is 10·91 ± ·01. The apparent division by both 5 and 6 is more satisfactory than appears at first sight, as all the $\frac{5}{6}$ths are found at one place, and it appears to be a purely local variation of the unit. If all the examples of $\frac{5}{6}$ths are rejected from the group, the mean is 10·89 ± ·01, so that it is nearly immaterial whether they are included or not. This unit appears to be the so-called "foot of Pliny" of 10·92, and the half of the Oriental cubit of 21·88 = 2 × 10·94.

(77) Another unit occurs in the following :—

		$\pm$			$\pm$
[6]Knidos, tomb	13·29	·03	1	13·29	·03
[18]Mura, theatre	22·17	·02	$\frac{3}{5}$	13·302	·012
[8]Assos, wall	8·31	·01	$\frac{5}{8}$	13·328	·016
[15]Telmissos, rock tomb . .	8·37	·01	$\frac{5}{8}$	13·392	·016
[22]Aizanoi theatre	13·415	·011	1	13·415	·011
[11]Pergamon, basilica . . .	8·387	·012	$\frac{5}{8}$	13·419	·019

Mean 13·36 ± ·02; this is a unit we have already found in Egypt and Syria, and is probably the so-called "foot of Drusus," reckoned at 13·1. The Stambouli cubit of 2 × 13·33 may be this same unit continued in the country.

(78) The next is a very clear and evident group :—

G

		$\pm$			$\pm$
[10]Patara, tomb	3·9646	·0024	1	3·9646	·0024
[7]Pergamon, bridge . . .	15·88	·02	4	3·970	·005
[2]Antiphellos, Lycian tomb .	·798	·001	$\frac{1}{5}$	3·990	·005
[6]Antiphellos, near sea . .	7·99	·02	2	3·995	·01
[4]Antiphellos, Doric tomb .	4·020	·012	1	4·020	·012
[28]Aspendos, theatre . . .	4·030	·003	1	4·030	·003

The mean is 3·994 ± 005.   5 × this unit is 19·97, which
is identical with the 19·97 of Assyria and other countries.

(79) The Olympic foot appears as follows :—

		$\pm$			$\pm$
[4]Cassaba, church	3·0175	·001	$\frac{1}{4}$	12·070	·004
[11]Ankura, Augusteum . .	16·13	·02	$\frac{4}{3}$	12·10	·02
[6]Iassos, camp of Leleges .	15·154	·007	$\frac{5}{4}$	12·123	·006
[3]Aizanoi bridge	10·12	·01	$\frac{5}{6}$	12·14	·01
[6]Aperlai, near theatre . .	4·860	·003	$\frac{2}{5}$	12·15	·01

The mean is 12·11 ± ·01. The multiples of the mean
unit found are not satisfactory, as they are so various,
implying a division by 4, 5, and 6. If the unit was one
hitherto unknown, I should probably have thought it too
dubious to be worth notice; and I certainly expected a
far larger number of instances of the Olympic foot, but
these are all that can possibly belong to it out of 70
remains examined.

(80) The Roman foot is perhaps found in two cases :—

		$\pm$			$\pm$
[11]B. M. Lycian tomb . . .	1·1637	·0014	$\frac{1}{10}$	11·637	·014
[14]Iassos, stadion	11·64	·01	1	11·64	·01

These are the only instances of the Roman foot yet
found in Asia Minor ; whether the unit was introduced
before the Roman conquest, must depend on the date to
be assigned to the remains. The B. M. Lycian tomb is
the unnamed fragment of a cornice imitating a roof of

poles. The Iassos stadion is given in Texier's Asie Mineure.

(81) The next is a compact group:—

	±		±	
[5]Trapezous, church of the Virgin Chrusokephalos .	15·39	·04	$\frac{4}{5}$	19·24	·05
[4]B. M. Knidos, term in socket	2·894	·004	$\frac{3}{20}$	19·29	·03
[8]Miletos, temple of Apollo .	19·29	·02	1	19·29	·02
[2]Iassos building	9·65	·02	$\frac{1}{2}$	19·30	·04
[2]B. M. Priene, temple of Athene	9·65	·02	$\frac{1}{2}$	19.30	·04
[11]Telmissos, rock tomb . .	6·442	·013	$\frac{1}{3}$	19·33	·04
[6]Knidos, tomb	9·760	·013	$\frac{1}{2}$	19·34	·03

The mean is 19·301 ± ·006 ; a similar unit is found in Egypt, Persia, and Africa, &c. It is apparently double the Pythic foot; 19·30 ÷ 2 = 9·650 ± ·003, and 9·75 is the value assigned to the Pythic foot.

(82) Another unit is found in eight remains :—

	±		±	
[7]Mura, church St. Nicolas .	5·339	·008	3	1·780	·003
[8]Arneai, Kuane, houses .	17·81	·03	10	1·781	·003
[11]Pergamon, bridge . . .	17·90	·03	10	1·790	·003
[9]Telmissos, Lycian tomb .	14·92	·02	$\frac{100}{12}$	1·790	·002
[11]Assos, city gate	28·68	·07	16	1·792	·004
[8]Mura, rock tomb . . .	2·689	·004	$1\frac{1}{2}$	1·793	·003
[8]Urgub, tomb	2·989	·002	$\frac{5}{3}$	1·793	·001
[21]Ankura, church	5·989	·008	$\frac{10}{3}$	1·797	·002

Mean 1·791 ± ·001 ; see next group.

(83) The only other Asiatic unit occurs in the following:—

	±		±	
[11]Alexandria Troas, gymnasium	27·78	·03	$\frac{100}{8}$	2·222	·003
[7]Nikaia, Lefke gate, A.D.130	11·13	·02	5	2·226	·004
[5]Aphrodisias, stadion . .	11·207	·001	5	2·2414	·0002
[3]Pessinous	4·484	·006	2	2·242	·003

The mean is 2·235 ± ·003. This *may* be connected with the preceding unit, 2·235 × 4 being 8·94 ± ·01, and 1·791 × 5 being 8·955 ± ·005; thus the probable errors of the two just connect them. This seems so far likely, that perhaps we may say 8·95 ± ·01 for both groups together. The ¼ of it, 2·235 × 5 = 11·175 ± ·015, which is a Phœnician foot, as we shall see farther on (106).

RESULTS.

(84) Thus the following are the units found inductively in Asia Minor, with the number of buildings in which I have yet noticed them :—

11 of 20·64	± ·02	divided decimally and binarily.
8 of 17·25	·02	divided decimally, ¹⁰⁄₁₂ths of 20·64; 1·730 in Persia.
5 of ·7330	·0004	digit.
13 of 1·885	·001	often used × 3 = 5·658 ± ·005; thus in Syria and Greece.
9 of 10·91	·01	"foot of Pliny" 10·92, and 21·88 cubit = 2 × 10·94.
6 of 13·36	·02	"foot of Drusus," 13·19 to 13·45, Egypt, Syria, Greece, &c.
6 of 3·994	·005	× 5 = 19·97 as in Assyria.
5 of 12·11	·01	Olympic foot.
2 of 11·64	·01	Roman foot.
7 of 19·301	·006	18·92 to 19·24 Egypt, &c. Double Pythic foot.
12 of 8·95	·01	once found in Greece. ¼ of it × 5 = Phœnician foot.

Thus out of eleven units found in Asia Minor, eight are historically known to have been used by nations that ruled there, and the other three are connected with units of adjacent countries.

GREECE.

(85) Under this head the Sicilian remains are included, as the civilisation under which they were executed was Greek in origin and in connections.

The following is a compound group, part being due to the use of the Roman foot under Imperial rule, and part to the use of a unit nearly identical with it used in the Kuklopeian remains:—

	Unit.	±		Mean unit.	±
[8]Epidauros promontory, columns	8·57	·03	$\frac{3}{4}$	11·43	·04
[5]Athens, columns near mon. of Lusikrates. . .	1·145	·001	$\frac{1}{10}$	11·45	·01
*[7]Tiruns, walls	23·04	·08	2	11·52	·04
*[9]B. M. Mukenai, sculpture	·2308	·0004	$\frac{1}{50}$	11·54	·02
[19]Epidauros, theatre in grove of Asklepios . .	2·317	·004	$\frac{1}{5}$	11·585	·02
*[8]Mukenai, treasury of Atreus	5·796	·018	$\frac{1}{2}$	11·59	·04
*[4]Mukenai, walls, &c. . .	11·60	·05	1	11·60	·05
*[3]Orchomenos, treasury of Minuas	18·6	·1	$\frac{8}{5}$	11·62	·06
†[9]Athens, aqueduct of Hadrian	4·357	·005	$\frac{3}{8}$	11·62	·01
[12]Thessalonike, Incantada .	11·64	·02	1	11·64	·02
*[6]Argos, pyramid	5·841	·008	$\frac{1}{2}$	11·68	·02
†[12]Athens, Pantheon of Hadrian	11·70	·01	1	11·70	·01
†[7]Athens, theatre of Herodes	17·562	·004	$\frac{3}{2}$	·11·708	·003
[11] Surakosai, theatre. . .	4·695	·003	$\frac{2}{5}$	11·74	·01

The mean of those marked *, which are certainly free from Roman influence in their design, is 11·60 ± ·02. This seems to be almost the sole Pelasgic or Kuklopeian unit; and it is the same as the "Ancient Greek foot" of 16 Egyptian digits, mentioned by some authors; 16 of the usual Egyptian digits would make it 11·64 ± ·02. Those examples marked † are very probably the Roman foot introduced under the Emperors; the mean of these is 11·68 ± ·02. The mean of the remaining examples, unmarked, which are perhaps the descended form of the Pelasgic unit, is 11·58 ± ·04. If all the post-Pelasgic remains are grouped together, their mean is 11·62 ± ·02; but there is such a probability of the Roman foot having been introduced in Imperial works, that those remains are better separated. The presence of $\frac{3}{2}$, $\frac{3}{4}$, and $\frac{3}{8}$ as variations of the unit is not surprising, as they are simply 1, $\frac{1}{2}$, and $\frac{1}{4}$ of a cubit of $1\frac{1}{2}$ feet, which is known to have been used by the Romans and Egyptians.

(86) The most usual Greek unit is the following :—

		±			±
[9]Thessalonike, St. Sophia .	12·26	·01	1	12·26	·01
[2]Elateia, temple of Pallas Kraneae	12·3 ?	·1	1	12·3?	·1
[8]Thessalonike, St. George .	30·78	·04	$2\frac{1}{2}$	12·312	·012
[2]B. M. Pelagonia, bust of Aischines	2·054	·04	$\frac{1}{6}$	12·324	·024
[7]Thessalonike, St. Elias . .	12·33	·016	1	12·33	·016
[6]B. M. Altar of Libations .	2 063	·03	$\frac{1}{6}$	12·38	·02
[9]Athens, temple of Triptolemos	4·649	·005	$\frac{3}{8}$	12·397	·012
[5]Delos, temple	12·40	·01	1	12·40	·01
[2]B. M. bust of Bacchos . .	3·101	·003	$\frac{1}{4}$	12·404	·012
[2]Ligurio, theatre	2·073	·002	$\frac{1}{6}$	12·44	·012
[20]Athens, propulaia . . .	12·44	·01	1	12·44	·01
[7]Segesta, temple	12·45	·015	1	12·45	·015
[7]Aigina, temple of Zeus Panhellenon	6·235	·007	$\frac{1}{2}$	12·470	·014
[14]Athena, Theseion . . .	9·375	·005	$\frac{3}{4}$	12·500	·006
[1]B. M. Phigaleia, frieze . .	12·573	·014	1	12·573	·014

The mean of this group is 12·40 ± ·01. The presence of $\frac{3}{4}$ and $\frac{3}{8}$ implies that a cubit was formed of $1\frac{1}{2}$ of these feet, these being $\frac{1}{2}$ and $\frac{1}{4}$ of the cubit. The three instances of $\frac{1}{6}$ being used suggests that this foot was divided into 6 spaces, on perhaps 12 thumbs, especially as the propulaia measures show $\frac{1}{12}$ths of this foot; now $12\cdot40 \div 6 = 2\cdot067 \pm \cdot02$, and we have already seen that the $20\cdot6$ cubit was divided decimally in Egypt and elsewhere; therefore it seems very probable that this foot is the duodecimal multiple of the usual decimal scale of the $20\cdot6$ cubit, especially as this same foot was adopted in Babylon by taking $\frac{2}{3}$ths of the $20\cdot6$ cubit.

(87) The following are examples of the Olympic foot :—

		±			±
[4]Nemea, Doric temple . .	18·207	·015	$\frac{3}{2}$	12·138	·010
[7]Messene, city gate . . .	6·079	·008	$\frac{1}{2}$	12·158	·016
[7]Delos, portico of Philip .	9·1200	·0085	$\frac{3}{4}$	12·160	·011
[5]Kastalian cistern	3·045	·003	$\frac{1}{4}$	12·180	·012

The mean is $12\cdot159 \pm \cdot004$. This agrees well with the measure from the Parthenon step, $12\cdot1375 \pm \cdot0003$; strange to say, the rest of the Parthenon will not at all agree with this foot; for but very few measures, and those only subordinate ones, are solved by it. Many other Athenian buildings were tried with the Olympic foot, to see whether there was any reason for discrediting the units inductively found, but the result was the same as with the Parthenon. The $\frac{2}{3}$ and $\frac{3}{4}$ of the foot, are the cubit and $\frac{1}{2}$ cubit.

(88) Another unit appears in five instances :—

		±			±
[3]B. M. Thebai, Thessalia, tablet	1·121	·001	1	1·121	·001
[8]Akragas, temple of Herakles	7·072	·01	$\frac{25}{4}$	1·1315	·0016
[3]Korinthos, temple . . .	1·132	·001	1	1·132	·001
[8]Messene, tower on wall .	3·406	·004	3	1·135	·001
[2]B. M. Krannon, Thessalia, tablet	1·138	·004	1	1·138	·004

The mean is 1·131 ± ·002. This × 5 = 5·655 ± ·01, and is apparently the same as the Asiatic 5·658 ± ·005.

(89) The next is probably a compound group :—

		$\pm$			$\pm$
[4]Thessalonike, St. Bardias .	12·815	·02	2	6·408	·01 ⎫
[9]Athens, gymnasium of Ptolemaios	3·206	·005	$\frac{1}{2}$	6·412	·01 ⎪
[16]Athens, monument of Lusikrates	25·672	·015	4	6·418	·004 ⎬
[15]Thessalonike, church (now Eski Djouma mosque) .	16·08	·015	$2\frac{1}{2}$	6·432	·003 ⎭
[15]Athens, temple of the winds	3·2465	·0024	$\frac{1}{2}$	6·493	·005
[3]Mukonos, altar	2·175	·003	$\frac{1}{3}$	6·525	·01
[4]Thorikos, Doric temple .	6·531	·004	1	6·531	·004
[5]Ilissos, bridge over . . .	10·565	·002	$\frac{8}{5}$	6·603	·001 ⎫
[13]Athens, gate of Agora . .	6·630	·006	1	6·630	·006 ⎪
[2]B. M. Sarcophagus . . .	3·320	·003	$\frac{1}{2}$	6·640	·006 ⎬
[18]Thessalonike, St. Demetrius	13·32	·01	2	6·660	·005 ⎭

It is hardly possible to suppose that these units all belong to one group; the range of a 25th of the whole amount is more than can be attributed to any unit. There is a compact group at 6·408 to 6·432, another at 6·603 to 6·660, and three units lying between these groups, which it is hard to deal with. Perhaps the best plan is to take the means of the two main groups, and allow a larger probable error to them, to cover the possibility of the three intermediates falling in either of the groups. The means of the two groups are 6·425 ± ·003, and 6·630 ± ·006; the probable errors may be reckoned as ·02, calling the means 6·43 ± ·02 and 6·63 ± ·02, to allow for the uncertainties of the case.

The 6·63 × 2 is 13·36 ± ·04, which seems identical with the Asia Minor 13·36 ± ·02. The 6·43 is $\frac{2}{3}$ of the Pythic foot, which is rated at 9·75 inches; 6·43 × 1$\frac{1}{2}$ being = 9·65 ± ·03.

(90) The following two are probably connected :—

	+		+
[16]Dramyssus, theatre . . .	10·125 ·02	4	2·531 ·005
[8]Cadachio, Corfu, temple .	2·540 ? ·002	1	2·540 ·002

The mean is 2·538 ± ·002; and this seems much like the 25·3 cubit, which was divided decimally, and in Persia was 25·34 ± ·02.

(91) The only other unit found in Greece, besides those already classified, is

[4]Eleusis, temple . . 17·885 ± ·01.

Half of this is 8·942 ± ·005, and 8·95 ± ·01 is frequently found as a unit in Asia Minor; the identity of these two needs no comment.

RESULTS.

(92) Thus the units found in Greece, with the number of instances yet found, are as follows :—

6 of 11·60 $\overset{+}{·02}$ Pelasgic remains. Decimally divided. "Ancient Greek foot."

5 of 11·58 ·04 Later remains } also × 1½ to form a cubit.
3 of 11·68 ·02 Romano-Greek }

15 of 12·40 ·01 × 1½ to form a cubit. 6 × 2·067 ± ·002. Babylonian foot.

4 of 12·159 ·004 × 1½ to form cubit. Olympic foot.

5 of 1·131 ·002 ⅕th of Asiatic 5·658 ± ·005.

4 of 6·43 ·02 ⅔ of 9·65 ± ·03; 9·75 = Pythic foot.

4 of 6·63 ·02 Half of Asiatic 13·36 ± 02.

2 of 2·538 ·002 $\frac{1}{10}$ of Persian Royal cubit.

1 of 17·885 ·01 Double the Asiatic 8·95 ± 01.

Here 12·16 and 11·60 are the Greek units recognised in literature; 2·538 and 12·4 are also generally recognised in civilisations bordering on the Greek; 6·43 is apparently derived from a well-known unit; and 6·63, 17·88, and 1·131 are identical with Asiatic units inductively found.

(93) The well-known Greek system of measures in connection with the Olympic 12·16 foot has more regularity in its composition than appears at first sight; and as this has been seldom or never noticed, it may be well to draw attention to it here.

There are two pure decimal systems which are connected duodecimally; the foot is the basis of the one:—

$$
\begin{aligned}
&100 \ \pi o\delta\eta s \\
={}&10 \ \kappa\alpha\lambda\alpha\mu o\iota \\
={}&1 \ \pi\lambda\epsilon\theta\rho o\nu
\end{aligned}
$$

The παλαιστη belongs to this series, being ¼ of the πους; and the πυγον also, the ⅛ of the καλαμος.

The other system is apparently based on the digit:—

$$
\begin{aligned}
&9600 \ \delta\alpha\kappa\tau\upsilon\lambda o\iota, \text{ or } 10{,}000 \text{ usual or old digits.} \\
={}&960 \ \lambda\iota\chi\alpha\iota \\
={}&100 \ o\rho\gamma\upsilon\iota\alpha\iota \\
={}&10 \ \alpha\mu\mu\alpha\iota \\
={}&1 \ \sigma\tau\alpha\delta\iota o\nu
\end{aligned}
$$

The σπιθαμη belongs to these, being ⅕ of the οργυια; and the πηχυς also, ⅖ of the οργυια.

Here there may be some doubt as to the connection of the two lowest terms of this series; but on looking at the digits of other countries, we never find a single example among them as high as the 96th of the Greek οργυια, which is ·7586 inches. The digit was in

		Inch.
Egypt	. . . .	·7276
Babylonia	. . . . . .	·7300
Persia	. . . .	·7339
Syria	. . . . ·721 to	·740
Early Greece	11·60 ÷ 16 =	·7250
Rome	. . 11·64 ÷ 16 =	·7275

Thus ·7284 is the mean of the digits of other countries, none of which approach to ·7586; and it seems improbable that Greece should have a digit very different from those of all other countries, and different from that shown by the ancient Greek foot. Also the Olympic cubit is very closely equal to (and probably derived from) an Egyptian unit noticed by Boeckh, which is clearly a length of 25 digits; thus the foot would be $\frac{2}{3} \times 25 = 16\frac{2}{3}$ digits— *i.e.*, 6 feet or 1 *orguia* to 100 digits. And farther, the $\frac{1}{100}$th of the *orguia* is ·72845 by the Parthenon foot (12·1375), or ·7295 ± ·02 by the value for the foot inductively found (12·16); so that the *orguia* is exactly 100 of the digits usually found in other countries.

It would therefore seem highly probable, as the $\frac{1}{100}$th of the *orguia* corresponds with the usual, or early Greek, digit; and as the Olympic cubit and foot was probably derived from an Egyptian cubit of 25 digits, each $= \frac{1}{100}$th of the *orguia;* that the Greek digit was originally similar to those of other countries, especially Egypt, from which the Olympic cubit and foot was derived. Also, that thus the digit completed a pure decimal system in 5 grades, culminated in the *stadion;* and that afterwards it was slightly altered, in order to accommodate it to a binary division of the Olympic foot; which, instead of containing 100 digits to the 6 feet, or 25 to the cubit, as in Egypt (*i.e.*, $16\frac{2}{3}$ digits to the foot), contained only 16 of the new digits, a change which might seem practically convenient, but which overthrew the pure decimal system originally established.

This change would seem to have been caused by the πους decimal scale obtaining an ascendency over the δακτυλος scale; and perhaps the date of this change may be pointed out by the Pelasgic remains being all in Ancient Greek feet of 16 original or Egyptian digits, and later remains, probably from about the fifth century B.C., mainly dropping this old Pelasgic foot, and largely adopting other units, probably owing to the change in the digit which made the Pelasgic foot inconvenient to use.

The ratio of 24 : 25 between the Roman and Olympic feet, so often mentioned in Metrology, is due to the Olympic foot being $\frac{1}{6}$th of a 100, or 16$\frac{2}{3}$, old digits; whereas the Roman and the Pelasgic foot had a binary relation, being 16 old digits; thus 16 : 16$\frac{2}{3}$: : 24 : 25; this ratio also appearing in the 9,600 new digits instead of 10,000 old digits.

CHAPTER VII.

ITALY, AFRICA, AND SARDINIA.

ITALY.

(94) UNDER this head the Roman remains found in Britain, Africa, and other countries, are included, as being Italian work, and therefore probably constructed with Italian units.

Of Etrurian remains, there are so few instances of several good measures of one monument, that I have been compelled to adopt a less strictly inductive method. As the use of a cubit of about two Roman feet by the Etruscans seems to be generally recognised, I have tried the measurements with this cubit throughout, and those that would not agree to it I have examined inductively to search for other units. Of the Etrurian measures that agree to the 23-inch cubit the following is the mean of the best :—

		$\pm$
[4]Etruria tombs, &c. . .	23·07	·06
and also		
[4]B. M. Chiusi cists . .	23·04	·02

So 23·05 ± ·03 may, perhaps, be best adopted. This is comparable with the double of the Pelasgic unit 23·20 ± ·04, the lowest instances of which are 23·04 and 23·08.

(95) On examining the residual measures that did not agree to the above unit, the following was the result from the best of them :—

	Unit.	±		Mean unit.	±
[11]Etruria, tombs, &c. . . .	24·93	·06	2	12·46	·03
[4]Tarquinii, Grotto Pompej .	62·18	·06	5	12·44	·01
[18]Saturnia, cromlech tombs .	18·67	·07	1½	12·45	·05

The last two are purely inductive. It is doubtful whether any unit was used in the Saturnia tombs; they certainly look unmetrical, and I can only say, *if* there was a unit, we have it here, apparently a cubit of 1½ feet. The close accordance with the Tarquinii and other measures goes far to render it likely.

This unit of 12·45 ± ·02 is apparently identical with the commonest Greek foot 12·40 ± ·01.

This same unit is often found in Britain, as the following group shows :—

		±			±
[2]B. M. Lincoln, tablet, Deæ Matres	2·057	·004	⅙	12·342	·024
[14]Chedworth Villa, circ. A.D. 80	12·38	·03	1	12·38	·03
[5]B. M. Altar	·3118	·00025	1/40	12·47	·01
[4]B. M. Caerleon, tablet, Val. Victor	3·1232	·0016	¼	12·493	·006
[3]B. M.Binstead, sarcophagus (rude, but accurate) . .	·835	·002	1/15	12·525	·03
[9]B. M. Harpenden, sarco- phagus	1·569	·003	⅛	12·552	·024

The mean is 12·45 ± ·03; this, as we have already seen, was derived from the 20·7 cubit, which unit is found in Gaul in the following two cases :—

		$\overset{+}{}$			$\overset{+}{}$
[7]Riez, baptistry	5·146	·014	¼	20·58	·06
[6]Vernegue, temple . . .	5·203	·006	¼	20·81	·02

The mean is 20·70 ± ·06 ; the previous British unit 12·45, ÷ 6 is = 2·075 ± ·005 ; and the old Italian gives the same 2·075 ± ·003. The concurrence of these quantities seems to show that the Romans had a long edition of the 20·6 cubit, perhaps we might say 20·74 ± ·04.

(96) The standard Roman foot is found oftener than any other unit. In Britain we have—

		$\overset{+}{}$			$\overset{+}{}$
[2]B. M. PIRI˙NIPR . . .	·720	·001	$\frac{1}{16}$	11·52	·017
[3]Bignor, block of stone . .	1·744	·002	$\frac{20}{3}$	11·63	·01
[8]Ickleton, building . . .	11·64	·02	1	11·64	·02
[3]Gurnard's Bay, villa . .	11·65	·02	1	11·65	·02
[3]B. M. Altar, horseman . .	1·166	·001	$\frac{1}{10}$	11·66	·01
[3]B. M. Lincoln, Pudens . .	2·918	·016	¼	11·67	·06
[11]Bisley	11·700	·016	1	11·700	·016
[9]Chesterford, villa . . .	11·72	·03	1	11·72	·03
[3]B. M. London, Classicianus	2·9304	·0016	¼	11·722	·006
[5]B. M. Saufeius	1·1744	·0025	$\frac{1}{10}$	11·744	·025

The following give half of the uncia ($\frac{1}{12}$ foot):—

	$\overset{+}{}$			$\overset{+}{}$		∴ for the foot.	
[4]B. M. Welling- borough . .	·9697	·0008	2	·4848	·0004	11·635	·010
[3]B. M. London, Minories . .	2·454	·003	5	·4907	·0006	11·777	·014

The mean of all is 11·68 ± ·01.

The African instances of the foot are as follows :—

		±			±
[4]Hydra, arch of Severus . .	11·45	·04	1	11·45	·04
[2]Hydra, old pillars . . .	2·89	·01	¼	11·56	·04
[8]Constantine, arch . . .	17·39	·02	1½	11·593	·014
[2]Setif, gate	29·0 ?	·1	2½	11·60?	·04
[5]Constantine, aqueduct . .	17·52	·02	1½	11·68	·013
[4]Announa, church ? . . .	23·55	·02	2	11·78	·01
[4]Constantine, building . .	23·59	·06	2	11·79	·03
[3]Mokthar, Corinthian arch .	11·8	·1	1	11·8	·1
[3]Djemila, building . . .	23·6?	·1·	2	11·8?	·1

The mean is 11·68 ± ·02. The close resemblance of
this to the British is curious, and it is strange that both
should be so far larger than the pure Roman foot
according to the best sources. The mean of 10 foot
rules preserved to us is 11·644 ± ·008, and this is exactly
the same as Boeckh's result, though from different data.
Our other sources of literary information concerning it
would not incline me to alter this result at all, as they
agree so well with it; perhaps 11·64 ± ·01 may be best
adopted as the final result for the pure Roman foot. The
colonial Roman seems to be longer, 11·68 ± ·01.

(97) The digit is found in four cases:—

		±			±
[2]Hydra, citadel	4372·	12·	600	7·287	·02
[5]Constantine, building . .	43·91	·06	6	7·318	·01
[4]Guelma, theatre	24·415	·018	1⁰⁄₃	7·324	·005
[10]Ghaareeah, arch	14·66	·02	2	7·33	·01

The mean is 7·320 ± ·002 for 10 digits; this agrees
fairly with the foot, as 16 of these digits are 11·712 ±
·003.

(98) The Olympic cubit occurs as follows :—

		±			±
[15]Woodchester, villa . . .	18·27	·03	1½	12·180	·020
[3]Westminster, sarcophagus	18·29	·02	1½	12·193	·013

An African agrees with these :—

		$\overset{+}{\cdot 3}$	25		$\overset{+}{\cdot 012}$
[2]Theveste, temple of Jupiter	303·4			12·136	

Thus the Olympic cubit used in Britain appears to be rather long, the foot being 12·19 ± ·01, whereas in Africa the one example agrees minutely with the Parthenon standard.

(99) A frequent African unit is as follows :—

		$\overset{+}{}$			$\overset{+}{}$
[4]Hydra, church	32·7	·2	2½	13·08	·08
[3]Scillitana	26·47	·08	2	13·24	·04
[3]Djemila	53·58	·05	4	13·395	·012
[4]Hydra, near church . . .	13·40	·02	1	13·40	·02
[4]Djemila	67·43	·01	5	13·486	·002
[9]Sufetula, arch and temples	13·57	·02	1	13·57	·02
[4]Eldjem, theatre	13·65	·01	1	13·65	·01

The mean is 13·45 ± ·03; and there seems to have been a native edition of this same unit, see (105). This seems to be the same as the Asia Minor unit 13·36 ± ·02.

(100) In Italy two units seem to coincide with two others in Britain, as the following show :—

		$\overset{+}{}$			$\overset{+}{}$
[8]Pola, theatre	4·270	·004	1	4·270	·004
[4]Heydon, villa	12·8	·1	3	4·27	·03
[2]B. M. Corbridge, altar . .	4·285	·008	1	4·285	·008
[10]Tusculum, reservoir . . .	4·31	·03	1	4·31	·03

This is a mongrel group, as to its localities; but all the remains are thoroughly Roman, except, perhaps, the altar. The mean is 4·275 ± ·003; this × 5 = 21·375 ± ·015 identical with a Persian, Assyrian, and Egyptian cubit.

(101) The following two may be connected :—

		±			±
[11]Pola, arch of Sergii . . .	3·990	·004	2	1·995	·002
[5]B. M. Southfleet, sarcopha-gus.	2·011	·011	1	2·011	·011

The mean is 1·996 ± ·002; this is curiously like $\frac{1}{10}$th of 19·97 ± ·04, an Assyrian unit.

(102) The following group is exclusively Romano-British :—

		±			±
[2]B. M. Lincoln, Faustina .	3·737	·004	5	·7475	·0008
[5]B. M. Altar	1·501	·004	2	·7506	·002
[4]B. M. Altar, Æsculapius .	4·515	·016	6	·7525	·0027
[9]B. M. Altar, Deo Marti .	1·506	·002	2	·753	·001

The mean is ·7500 ± ·0008, a long digit.

(103) The following are isolated units, only found in one monument :—

		±	
[7]Pola, temple	5·304	·003	
[2]Auriol, St. Peter	335·9	·4	
[5]Beddington, villa	7·421	·007	10 long digits.
[2]B. M. Benwell, tablet . . .	1·897	·001	
[2]Setif, mills	4·6 ?	·2	
[2]Setif, vaulted chambers . .	56·7 ?	·4	

RESULTS.

(104) The Italian units, then, are as follows, the prefixed number being the number of examples found :—

	±		
10 of 23·05	·03	Etruria.	Pelasgic unit.
14 of 12·45	·02	Etruria.⎫	20 of 12·45 ± ·02. Græco-Baby-
6 of 12·45	·03	Britain. ⎭	lonian foot.
2 of 20·70	·06	Gaul.	Royal Egyptian cubit.
12 of 11·68	·01	Britain.⎫	21 of 11·68 ± ·01. Roman foot.
9 of 11·68	·02	Africa. ⎭	
4 of 7·320	·002	Africa.	10 digits.

2 of	12·19	·01	Britain.	
1 of	12·14	·01	Africa.	ε of 12·17 ·02. Olympic foot.
7 of	13·45	·03	Africa. Asiatic "Drusian foot."	
4 of	4·275	·003	× 5 = 21·375. Egypto-Assyrio-Persian cubit.	
2 of	1·996	·002	× 10 = 19·96. Assyria and Asia Minor.	
4 of	·7500	·0008	a long digit. ·7491 ± ·003 long Egyptian digit.	

Of these 20·70, 11·68, 7·32, and 12·17 are all well known; 23·05 is probably identical with the double 11·6. 12·45, 13·45, 1·996 (× 10), 4·275 (× 5), and ·7500 are the same as units we have already observed in other countries.

AFRICA.

(105) We have already referred to one African unit, akin to a Romano-African that has been detailed (99).

	Unit.	±		Mean unit.	±
[1][6]Mauretania, Royal tomb .	6·617	·01	½	13·23	·02
[2]Sigus, cromlech	66·7	·2	5	13·34	·04
[5]Utica, chambers	13·51	·03	1	13·51	·03

The mean is 13·34 ± ·05. On the cromlech, see (146).

(106) Another African unit is found at Carthage only :—

		±	
[8]Cisterns	11·163	·006	⎫ Mean
[4]Temple of Æsculapius	11·166	·003	⎬ 11·165
[3]Aqueduct	11·20	·06	⎭ ±·002

This may be 15 digits of 7·443 ± ·001 each; and what renders this very probable is that this Punic unit is about equal to the digit of Bashan, ·7400 ± ·0015 (see 61), which is apparently × 15 or 30 in the example of it that we have; thus the Bashan foot was 11·10 ± ·02, and was, perhaps, derived from the Phœnicians. A unit of Asia Minor, 2·235 ± ·003 (83), when × 5 is = 11·17 ± ·015, which is also much like the Phœnician foot.

(107) Two other units are at present unconnected with any group owing to the paucity of the Punic measures :—

		±
[7]Carthage, temple of Baal	11·74	·06
[5]Moghrawa, building	9·62	·03

11·74 may be the same as the Pelasgo-Etrurian foot. 9·62 (× 2 = 19·24 ± ·06) appears to be the Pythic foot, also found in Asia Minor, Persia, and Egypt.

SARDINIA.

(108) The materials are but scanty, and somewhat rough; but still, so far as they go, the following units have been obtained from the probably non-Roman remains. The following is the most frequent unit :—

	Unit.	±		Mean unit.	±
[3]Perda Lunga	22·12	·02	16	1·382	·001
[8]Noraghe Vois	55·34	·2	40	1·384	·005
[6]Noraghe Barile	4·168	·007	3	1·389	·002
[4]Noraghe Santinu	27·8	·1	20	1·390	·005

These agree closely, and their mean is 1·384 ± ·001. This was evidently binarily multiplied, 16, 40, and 20 show this; and if × 8 it is 11·07 ± ·01, giving 2, 5, and 2½ for the multiples above. Probably this is the same as the Punic foot, 11·165 ± ·002.

(109) The next three appear to be connected :—

	±			±
[2]Noraghe Ortu	81·2 ·2	24	3·384	·008
[5]Noraghe Sta. Barbara . .	13·58 ·03	4	3·395	·007
[11]Perda S' Altare	8·51 ·01	2½	3·404	·004

These also agree very closely; the mean is 3·399 ± ·003.

(110) Another unit may occur in—

	±			±	Mean
[2]Fontana Nuova	197·0 ·5	10	19·70	·05	19·74
[2]Noraghe Oës	19·78 ·05	1	19·78	·05	± ·03

(111) The next two apparently give another unit :—

	±			±
[5]Tamuli, broken stele . . .	7·58 ·03	4	1·895	·007
[3]Lintel of Noraghe . . .	9·48 ·01	5	1·896	·002

These agree most remarkably; the mean is 1·896 ± ·002; this resembles the Egyptian 18·92 ± ·02 and similar units in Asia and Africa.

(112) One other unit occurs in—

	±			±	Mean
[5]Cippus	2·155 ·013	⅕	10·77	·07	10·80
[5]Sepoltura, stele	10·85 ·1	1	10·85	·1	± ·02

(113) The following are isolated examples :—

	±
[5]Noraghe di Alvu	20·08 ·02
[2]Sant' Antioco, "Del Prato"	29·53 ·02
[5]The "Altare"	13·26 ·05

20·08 resembles the 19·97 unit of Italy and other countries. 29·53 is probably 10 palms, of which 7 form a cubit of 20·671 ± ·014. 13·26 is identical with the frequent unit in Egypt, Greece, Italy, &c., of 13·2 to 13·4.

It will be observed that the Noraghe are grouped
by identity of unit, along with other remains—the
Sepolturas, and rude stone monuments; thus implying
that all these remains are due to one race, according
to the evidence of measures.

RESULTS.

(114) Thus the Sardinian units are—

$$\pm$$

4 of 1·384 ·001 × 8 = 11·07 ± ·01, Punic foot.
3 of 3·399 ·003
2 of 19·74 ·03
2 of 1·896 ·002 × 10 = 18·96 ± ·02, Egyptian, &c.
2 of 10·80 ·02   × 2 = 21·60 ± ·04, Assyria, Egypt, Italy.
1 of 20·08 ·02   19·96, Italy and Asia.
1 of 29·53 ·02   10 palms of the 20·67 cubit.
1 of 13·26 ·05   13·2 to 13·4, Egypt, Greece, Italy, &c.

So that 6 units are known in adjacent countries and
civilisations, and two—*i.e.*, 3·339 and 19·74—seem to be
new units.

CHAPTER VIII.

MEDIÆVAL IRELAND AND ENGLAND.

OF mediæval remains I have only examined those of England and Ireland for units of measure; those on the Continent will afford a rich harvest when examined, as they will illustrate the descent of modern European units, and probably throw much light on the tribal history and connections of the Dark Ages.

IRELAND.

(115) The Irish remains will be here considered first, as those examined are of earlier date than the generality of English buildings.

The commonest unit is as follows:—

	Unit.	±		Mean unit.	±
[3]Killaloe, church, 639 A.D. .	70·4 ?	·4	16	4·40 ?	·03
[7]Glendalough, gateway . .	4·41	·02	1	4·41	·02
[2]St. Benen, oratory . . .	44·5 ?	1·	10	4·45 ?	·1
[4]St. Kevin's, chancel . . .	8·95 ?	·05	2	4·47 ?	·03
[4]Tirerill, Aghamagh, church	4·48	·02	1	4·48	·02
[3]Glendalough, round tower	22·4 ?	·2	5	4·48?	·04
[2]Donaghmore	9·0 ? ?	·05	2	4·50 ? ?	·03
[3]Clonmacnoise	9·0 ? ?	·05	2	4·50 ? ?	·03
[6]Rattoô, round tower . . .	9·05 ?	·1	2	4·52 ?	·05

Many of these are dubious, as the measures were but poor for the purpose. The mean is 4·46 ± ·01.

(116) Another group is rather wide in extent:—

		$\pm$			$\pm$
[6]Oratory of Gallerus . . .	5·58	·04	1	5·58	·04
[5]Lough Lee, St. Finan's house	5·655	·01	1	5·655	·01
[4]Drumbo, round tower . .	34·0 ?	·1	6	5·67	·02
[3]Kells, St. Columba's house	11·4 ?	·05	2	5·70	·03
[3]St. Fechin's house . . .	28·57	·15	5	5·71	·03
[4]Ardoilen, church	17·2 ? ?	·1	3	5·73	·03

The mean is 5·67 ± ·01.

(117) The following group together :—

		$\pm$			$\pm$
[4]Ratass, Tralee, church . .	5·29	·03	1	5·29	·03
[5]Inchaguile, Galway, church	53·3	·1	10	5·33	·01
[10]Clondalkin, round tower .	10·66	·03	2	5·33	·02
[9]St. Kevin's house . . .	10·72	·02	2	5·36	·01
[8]Glendalough	16·2 ? ?	·2	3	5·4	·1
[2]Temple Connor, church .	108· ?	·1	20	5·4	·05
[2]St. Gobnet's oratory . .	54·	2·	10	5·4	·2

The mean is 5·34 ± ·01.

(118) The next four are, perhaps, related :—

		$\pm$			$\pm$
[8]Isle of Aran, Galway bay, church	16·6	·1	4	4·15	·03
[5]Kilmacduagh, St. Fechan, 664 A.D.	4·24	·02	1	4·24	·02
[7]Clonmacnoise, Fineen's church	21·67	·13	5	4·33	·05
[3]Antrim, round tower . .	4·35	·02	1	4·35	·02

The mean is 4·27 ± ·03.

(119) These four mean units are all closely connected ; whether by origin or accident the facts will best show :—

Mean units.			Base.	$\pm$
4 of 4·27 ·03	÷ 12 =		·3558	·0025
9 of 4·46 ·01	$\frac{25}{2}$		·3568	·0008
7 of 5·34 ·01	15		·3560	·0007
6 of 5·67 ·01	16		·3544	·0007

Thus the probable errors of these units almost all overlap each other, and the mean value of the base is

·3556 ± ·0003. This is the simplest way to consider
their relationship, though, of course, it is not intended
to imply that they were derived from so small a unit
as ·35 inch; but this is a convenient basis to which to
reduce them for comparison. It would seem very
likely, on viewing these units, that 60 × this base
was the original unit—*i.e.,* 21·34 ± ·02; this divided
sexagesimally and decimally would, of course, easily
result in each of the mean units above. Thus in the
present state of information nothing better can be stated
than that a unit of 21·34 ± ·02 (÷ 60) was an original
basis from which other units were found.

(120) The following three seem to be connected:—

	±		±	
[7]Glendalough, chapel . .	9·771	·005	2	4·885	·003
[9]Glendalough, church . .	9·805	·02	2	4·902	·010
[3]Iniscaltra, 7th cent.. . . .	123·?	2·	25	4·92	·08

The mean is 4·890 ± ·005.

(121) The following are apparently unconnected
with any other units:—

		±
[4]Rahin, church, 8th cent.	7·91	·03
[2]Tomb of St. Muireadach	19·0?	·4
[2]Teampull, oratory	46·7?	·5

We may, therefore, conclude that 21·34 ± ·02 (÷ 60)
and 4·890 ± ·005 are the Christian Irish units. It is
worth notice that the round towers are completely
mixed with the churches in the groups, in unison with
the soundest views as to their origin; all the towers
examined having the 21·34 unit.

ENGLAND.

(122) This section of the subject has been more

examined than most others; the English churches and other mediæval buildings affording such ample materials. About 70 of the buildings mentioned have been carefully measured by myself, and are marked by an asterisk against the probable errors, as showing that the error is due to workmanship, and not to measurement; also in these cases the parts selected were those that were likely to be metrical. Ch. is put for church, and + for the stone crosses. The dates are given by centuries (C^{14}, C^{15}, &c.), but they are in most cases merely guesses, which do not profess any particular accuracy; and I do not wish for a moment to uphold them, if any authority decides otherwise: the object of giving them being just to prevent a unit of a Norman building being attributed to Tudor date, or any such gross uncertainty; but they are probably as accurate as can be required in the present state of metrology.

The following are the examples of the inch and foot that has survived all others, and continued in use among us:—

		Unit.	$\pm$		Mean unit.	$\pm$
[2]Puttenham ch. brass, 1438 .		·9842	·0003	1	·9842	·0003*
[4]Eynesford castle . . .	C^{12}	11·87	·05	12	·9890	·0040*
[9]Eltham bridge . . .	C^{14}	11·896	·006	12	·9913	·0005*
[14]Portchester castle, baillie	C^{14}	·992	·002	1	·992	·002*
[4]Sompting ch., N. door .	C^{12}	11·944	·015	12	·9957	·0013*
[3]Tisbury + ...	C^{15}	11·96	·01	12	·9973	·0008*
[6]Chideock ch. tower . .	C^{14}	11·967	·013	12	·997	·001*
[8]Weston +, Dartford . . .		11·98	·05	12	·999	·004*
[2]Tisbury, Foyle tomb, 1641 .		12·006	·016	12	1·0005	·0014*
[3]Abbotsleigh + . . .	C^{15}	12·02	·05	12	1·002	·004
[25]Abbotsbury,St.Catharine's	C^{15}	12·043	·008	12	1·0036	·0007*
[5]Sherborne minster, W. door .		6·035	·005	6	1·006	·001*
[7]Shaftesbury + . . .	C^{15}	12·09	·02	12	1·0075	·0017*
[7]Portchester ch. transepts	C^{12}	18·15	·09	18	1·008	·005*
[3]Witley ch., Surrey, S. door	C^{12}	10·10	·03	10	1·010	·003*
[7]Hamble ch.	C^{12}	1·013	·002	1	1·013	·002*

The mean of these is ·9998 ± ·0011; from this it seems that the inch now in use, has not varied any appreciable amount, on the average, for centuries.

(123) The next is the most usual English unit :—

		±			±
[3]Worth, Sussex, sepulchral slab . . . . . C[14]	8·69	·04	$\frac{2}{3}$	13·035	·08
[1]Whittington +, Glostershire . . . . . C[15]	13·1		1	13·1	
[8]Mayfield ch. and hall C[14]	13·12	·02	1	13·12	·02
[13]Hayes ch., Kent . . C[12]	8·764	·016	$\frac{2}{3}$	13·146	·024*
[2]Badgworth +, Glostershire C[15]	13·15	·02	1	13·15	·02
[2]Sapperton +, Glostershire	13·15	·04	1	13·15	·04
[7]St. Mary Cray ch., N. door	13·16	·02	1	13·16	·02*
[10]Portchester ch., W. door C[12]	4·390	·004	$\frac{1}{3}$	13·17	·01*
[6]Bilbury ch. . . Saxon	8·80	·03	$\frac{2}{3}$	13·20	·05
[30]Southampton W. gate and wall . . . . . C[13]	13·20	·02	1	13·20	·02*
[5]Tisbury ch., W. door. C[13]	1·320	·012	$\frac{1}{10}$	13·20	·12*
[2]Warwick castle . . C[14]	13·2	·1	1	13·2	·1
[8]Stone ch., Dartford, N. door C[12]	13·22	·03	1	13·22	·03*
[1]Brookthorpe + . . C[13]	13·25		1	13·25	
[4]Lewes castle (part) . . .	13·255	·008	1	13·255	·008
[2]Stokesay castle . . C[13]	53·10	·04	4	13·27	·01
[4]Eastleach + . . . C[15]	13·29	·04	1	13·29	·04
[11]Southampton, N.W. walls C[14]	13·32	·02	1	13·32	·02*
[3]Higham, Kent, sepulchral slab . . . . . C[15]	13·47	·07	1	13·47	·07
[3]Kelmscott + . . . C[14]	13·5	·1	1	13·5	·1
[1]Westbury +, Glostershire C[12]	13·5		1	13·5	

The mean of these, omitting the three cases of one single measure each, is 13·22 ± ·01.

(124) The next is the most usual Saxon unit :—

		±			±
[9]Stone ch., Kent . Saxon ?	12·36	·03	1	12·36	·03*
[4]Lincoln castle	8·24	·02	$\frac{2}{3}$	12·36	·03
[4]Sompting ch., S. door C[12]	12·396	·016	1	12·396	·016*
[3]Lewes, lead box . . C[14]	2·075	·003	$\frac{1}{6}$	12·45	·02*
[2]Westcote +, Glostershire C[13]	12·5 ?	·2	1	12·5 ?	·2
[2]Coggeshall, chapel near, Saxon ?	12·5	·1	1	12·5	·1
[10]Deerhurst ch. . . Saxon	12·57	·03	1	12·57	·03
[5]Bermondsey, chalk-lined grave . . . . Saxon ?	12·62	·04	1	12·62	·04
[4]Tredington +, Glostershire C[14]	12·62	·03	1	12·62	·03
[3]Maiden Newton + . . .	2·540	·006	$\frac{1}{5}$	12·70	·03*

The mean is 12·47 ± ·03.

(125) Another group is formed thus :—

		±	
[3]Great Orme's Head, chapel . C[15]	7·74	·05	
[5]Hamble ch. N. porch . . . C[16]	7·746	·011*	Mean
[2]Stow-on-the-Wold + ...	7·79	·01	7·804
[9]Southampton N.W. wall courses C[15]	7·80	·03*	± ·008
[3]Hatherop + ... late C[14]	7·82	·01	
[20]Rothersthorpe ch., Yorks	7·857	·006	

(126) The next unit was continued to a late date :—

		±	
[2]Puttenham ch. brass . . . 1693	12·90	·02*	
[2]Durham cath., W. wing . . 1300	12·90	·04	
[2]Durham cath., room . . . 1090	12·92	·05	Mean
[3]Bromley ch., Kent, tomb . . 1674	12·93	·03*	12·97
[4]Durham, 9 altars 1240	12·99	·01	± ·01
[2]Newport ch., Essex, chest . . C[13]	13·0	·2	
[4]Witley ch., Surrey, brass . 1634	13·02	·03*	

(127) The next is a Western group :—

		±			±
[5]Maiden Newton ch., W. door . . . . . C[13]	3·960	·012	½	7·92	·02*
[4]Maiden Newton ch., N. door . . . . C[12]	·796	·001	$\frac{1}{10}$	7·96	·01*
[2]Bakewell ch., tomb, Saxon	8·0 ?	·1	1	8·0 ?	·1
[2]Cirencester + . . C[14]	8·0	·1	1	8·0	·1
[7]Llan Tysilio ch. . . C[13]	8·02 ?	·02	1	8·02 ?	·02

The mean is 7·96 ± ·01.

(128) The following is a South-eastern group :—

		±			±
[14]Netley Abbey, S.E. buildings	2·3104	·0022	$\frac{1}{5}$	11·55	·01*
[3]Dartford ch. font . . C[13]	11·57	·05	1	11·57	·05*
[3]Willingdon, Sussex, lead box C[11]	11·6	·2	1	11·6	·2
[2]Witley ch., Surrey, brass 1641	11·63	·02	1	11·63	·02*
[4]Dartford ch. tower . C[13]	11·74	·03	1	11·74	·03*

Mean 11·60 ± ·02.

(129) Another unit is as follows :—

		±	
[4]Llanfihangel ch. . . . . . . C[14]	8·40	·03	
[38]Netley Abbey ch.	8·460	·006*	Mean 8·458
[3]Ipswich, St. Peter's ch. font . . .	8·47	·03	± ·005
[5]Lewes, leaden cists . . . . C[14]	8·50	·06	

(130) The next four appear to belong together :—

		±			±
[11]Knowlton ch. aisle and porch	2·027	·005	$\frac{3}{10}$	6·757	·017*
[5]Chideock ch., S. porch C[15]	6·804	·006	1	6·804	·006*
[8]Eltham ch., W. door . C[14]	6·866	·01	1	6·866	·01*
[17]Knowlton ch. . . . C[13]	6·952	·006	1	6·952	·006*

The mean is 6·871 ± ·025.

(131) The last group is :—

			$\overset{+}{}$	
[3]Charlton Kings + ...	C[15]	12·16	·01	⎫ Mean
[6]Tortworth +.	C[14]	12·19	·03	⎬ 12·17
[5]Hayes ch., slabs of brasses .	C[17]	12·24	·03	⎭ ± ·01

(132) The remainder of the English units, under ⅖ths of the whole examined, are unfortunately still ungroupable. There are evidently some units which are not very different one from the other, and at present there are not sufficient data collected to disentangle them with certainty, as their variations nearly extend over the interval between them. When more examples of units shall be deduced from English remains, then, by being enabled to classify the variations of each unit, according to dates and localities, this uncertainty may be cleared away. For the present the best course seems to be to give here some rough idea of what the entangled units probably are, and of the number of buildings in which each occurs, as follows :—

	$\overset{+}{}$		
4 of 10·32	·01	Glostershire.	⎫
5 of 10·50	·01	Saxon and onward.	⎬ all connected?
4 of 10·65	·01	Kent and Sussex.	⎭
9 of 10·805	·005		
8 of 11·24			

4 of 14·22	·02
7 of 14·48	·01
8 of 14·68	·01
2 of 14·995	·008

RESULTS.

(133) The following are the mean units found in Mediæval England, and the number of cases in which each has been found; I have ventured to add, as suggestions, some units of other countries, which may —through Roman colonists and artificers, and other

sources—have been the prototypes of our English measures :—

16 of	·9998	·0011	1·996 ÷ 2 = ·998 ± ·001 Romano-British, &c.
21 of	13·22	·01	13·19 to 13·45 Egypt, Asia, Greece, and Rome.
10 of	12·47	·03	12·45 ± ·02 Romano-British, &c.
6 of	7·804	·008	
7 of	12·97	·01	
5 of	7·96	·01	1·996 × 4 = 7·984 ± ·008 Romano-British, &c.
5 of	11·60	·02	11·64 ± ·01 Roman foot (used in Britain).
4 of	8·458	·005	
4 of	6·871	·025	
3 of	12·17	·01	12·19 ± ·01 Romano-British, Olympic foot.

besides some other units between 10·3 and 11·2, and between 14·22 and 15·0.

From the known presence of five of these units in England during Roman times, the origin of these same units (or halves or doubles of them) as found in mediæval times may perhaps be derived. Another of the units, 13·22, is often found in Roman remains, though not yet found in Britain. For the remaining four units no origin is yet apparent. It must not be thought that these connections of the mediæval with classical units are mentioned with the same confidence as the connections between units of different classical countries ; they are, on the contrary, only given as possibilities worth notice, and the closeness of the connection is the best claim they can show. That units used by the Britons should be transmitted to the Anglo-Saxons is far from impossible, as the latter probably imbibed much of the fragmentary civilisation that they found in the Romano-Britons; early history relates the wars, and not the truces, of nations. That the Saxon units should descend to mediæval times is most probable, as the Normans were a ruling, and not a working, class.

CHAPTER IX.

RUDE STONE REMAINS, AMERICA, INDIA, &c.

RUDE STONE REMAINS AND EARTHWORKS.

(134) WE now come to a class of remains for which, judging by their appearance, I should hesitate to claim any metricality. I can hardly expect those who are familiar with the cromlechs, and the far-stretching green banks, found here and there over the country, to concede anything beyond a possibility of their preserving to us units of measure. I certainly should not have granted more myself, before I had any real grounds for judging of the matter; but having examined some of these remains with a view to their metricality, the tables seemed turned, and there certainly appears now to be a probability of the more regular remains being made by a measure-using people.*

If a difficulty in research is experienced from the roughness of the measures made of highly-finished buildings, how much more difficulty is found in using measures of rude remains, of which the traveller or the antiquary

---

* A paper " On Prehistoric Measures," by R. v. Luschin, was read at the *Naturforscher Versammlung* meeting in 1875; but as none of the proceedings are in the British Museum, and I could not obtain them from the principal German bookseller in London, I cannot avail myself of that paper.

thinks he has said enough, if he but describes them by pacing and guesswork, with " about" put to every item. This difficulty is not so serious as it seems at first sight, as we can use rather rougher measures of these rude remains than of more polished monuments; for we need not expect, or look for, fractions of a unit, or complex numbers; 2, 4, 8, 10, or 20 are the sort of multiples that we may expect, if there are any to be found.

(135) When we look at the following measures, we see at a glance that there is evidently something beyond mere chance lengths given here :—

Cromlech, Cloyne, Cork . . . 15 × 7 to 8 × 3½ feet.
Stone near St. Helier . . . . 14 × 7½ × 3 feet.
Arthur's stone, Cefn Bryn . . 14 × 7ft. 2in.

These lengths are plainly doubles of each other, and their recurrence in different monuments (of which I could give other examples) is beyond the probabilities of mere coincidence.

Again, when we find that two rude stone circles near each other in Dorsetshire, one of 980 ± 20 inches, and another of 323 ± 6 inches across,* are to each other exactly as 1 : 3, far within the limit of their probable error of workmanship (being in the ratio of 1 : 3·04 ± ·08) ; it is but reasonable to pause, and look at other remains to see if they will give similar evidence, when we condescend to examine them.

Many other instances of similarities might be quoted here to the same effect, but I will now proceed to point out such remains as appear to give the same unit when inductively examined; premising that every unit mentioned was obtained (as in the previous results) solely

* Gorwell and Winterbourne Abbas circles, according to very accurate plans.

from the monument to which it is here placed, and that no trials were made with a unit to see if it would fit to any of these remains ; but each monument was examined by itself, and its unit obtained purely by induction from the measures of it. If any unit exists in the following remains, we have it here stated ; but I certainly do not consider that the units found have such a probability of correctness in individual cases as those deduced from classical remains.

As there are very few accurate plans of ancient earthworks for reference, even in the British Museum, I have found it requisite to make many such plans myself. Only those remains that show some regularity, and are not bound by natural features of the ground, have been surveyed. Copies of the plans (of which there are some 30 or 40) are now deposited in the British Museum Map Department ; they are numbered No. $\frac{1\,1\,1\,2}{2\,8\,0\,0}$, and can be referred to by any reader (see 184). The remains to which an asterisk is appended in the following lists, are those given from my own plans and measurements.

(136) The following are the examples of the most frequently recurring unit. S shows that the unit is from the *dimensions* of a stone ; SS from the *positions* of stones ; E from dimensions of an earthen bank or mound ; EE from positions of earthworks (see 24).

FRANCE.

		Unit.	±		Mean unit.	±
[5]Grotto D'Esse . . .	SS	21·01	·04	1	21·01	·04
[1] Various remains not at Carnac	SS	21·3	·1	1	21·3	·1
[3]Logatjar	SS	53·4	·2	2½	21·36	·08
[3]Bourgon in Melle .	SS	42·8	·1	2	21·4	·05
[8]Kerlescant	SS	3434·	7·	160	21·46	·05
[7]Erdeven	SS	32·34	·07	1½	21·56	·05
[3]Jersey, St. Heliers . .	S	43·4	·8	2	21·7	·4

ENGLAND AND WALES.

			±			±
[5]Sussex, Bow Hill	EE	418·7	1·6	20	20·93	·08*
[3]Wilts, Silbury Hill	E	630·	2·	30	21·00	·07
[4]Dorset, Holly Down . . .	EE	63·25	·25	3	21·08	·08*
[5]Dorset, Tarrant Hinton .	EE	3172·	16·	150	21·14	·12*
[2]Glamorgan, Cefn Bryn . . .	S	85·5	·5	4	21·37	·1
[4]Somerset, Stoney Littleton	SS	21·44	·03	1	21·44	·03
[3]Dorset, Cerne Trendle Hill	EE	64·9	·2	3	21·63	·07*
[15]Cornwall, Castle An Dinas	SS	108·2	·4	5	21·64	·08
[7]Dorset, Moigne's Down, barrows	EE	217·	1·	10	21·7	·1*
[9]Dorset, Bincombe, barrows	EE	544·	1·	25	21·76	·04*
[8]Dorset, Black Down, barrow .	E	54·48	·07	2½	21·79	·03*
[7]Dorset, Bincombe, barrows	EE	290·6	·8	4·0/8	21·79	·06*
[6]Neolithic weapons, very fine .	S	2·18	·03	1/10	21·8	·3
[4]Kent, Kits Cotty House . .	S	21·88	·07	1	21·88	·07*
[7]Dorset, Cerne, by stream .	EE	438·	1·	20	21·90	·05*

SCOTLAND.

			±			±
[3]Battlemoss, lines . .	SS	63·85	·04	3	21·28	·01
[1]Garrywhin, lines . .	SS	257·		(12?)	21·4?)	
[5]Camster, lines . . .	SS	64·5	·6	3	21·5	·2
[2]Ring of Bookan . .	EE	540·	3·	25	21·6	·1

The mean of the French is 21·32 ± ·05; English, 21·48 ± ·06; Scotch, 21·34 ± ·04. · · ·

(137) The next group is one that might be confounded with the preceding on a rough view, but it is clearly distinct and separate in every country, for there is always a well-marked gap between the lengths in the two groups; and, moreover, these gaps correspond to each other in France, S.W. England, S.E. England, and Scotland. Thus we must consider that there were two pre-historic units of not very dissimilar values :—

FRANCE.

				±			±
[8]Landaoudec	SS	674·	1·	30	22·47	·03
[3]Pierres Plattes, Locmariaker .	S	34·	·1	1½	22·67	·07
[2]Carnac, Mont St. Michel . .	E	22·8	·1	1	22·8	·1

ENGLAND.

				±			±
[2]Hants, Abshot	S	22·2	·2	1	22·2	·2*
[3]Sussex, N.E. of Mt. Caburn	EE	222·3	·3	10	22·23	·03*
[4]Dorset, Little Ball . . .	EE	178·	1·	8	22·25	·12*
[2]Dorset, Gorwell, Hunebed	SS	178·	3·	8	22·25	·4*
[2]Dorset, Black Down, barrows	EE	222·6	·3	10	22·26	·03*
[10]Dorset, Came Down, barrows	EE	223·3	·4	10	22·33	·04*
[4]Devon, Grimspound . . .	SS	67·0	·1	3	22·33	·03
[5]Land's End, cromlechs . . .	S	56·3	3	2½	22·52	·12
[14]Dorset, Bincombe Down, barrows	EE	340·0	·5	15	22·67	·03*
[6]Dorset, Lambert's castle, inside	EE	56·9	·1	2½	22·76	·04*
[11]Dorset, Cerne, below Trendle Hill, barrows within square banks	EE	228·3	·7	10	22·83	·07*

SCOTLAND AND IRELAND.

				±			±
[16]Brough of Clickimin . .	SS	11·18	·04	½	22·36	·08
[16]Glen Columbkill, cromlechs .	S	11·24	·04	½	22·48	·08
[8]Maeshowe	SS	22·5	·3	1	22·5	·3
[16]Seanhinny	S	22·55	·07	1	22·55	·07
[4]Latheron, circle	SS	339·	1·	15	22·60	·07
[9]Glen Malin, cromlechs . . .	S	11·33	·04	½	22·66	·08

The mean of the French is 22·56 ± ·04, English 22·42 ± ·05, Scotch 22·53 ± ·03.

The following Irish objects probably belong to this group, but their probable errors are so large that they are uncertain :—

		±			±
[9]Bronze weapons, &c. . .	2·20	·03	$\frac{1}{10}$	22·0	·3
[3]Cloyne, Cork, cromlech . S	44·0	·6	2	22·0	·3

(138) The following units appear to form a group:—

		±			±
[16]Dorset, Cerne, Trendle Hill square . . . . . EE	40·8	·1	2	20·40	·05*
[5]Dorset, Blandford, long barrow . . . . EE	204·	1·	10	20·4	·1*
[3]Dorset, Stowerpaine . EE	512·	3·	25	20·48	·12*
and perhaps					
[4]Dartmoor, Hembury castle EE	10·35	·03	$\frac{1}{2}$	20·70	·06

The mean of the Dorset examples is 20·41 ± ·04.

(139) Another group of wide distribution is:—

		±			+
[6]Sussex, terrace ridges, near Mt. Caburn . . . EE	916·	5·	200	4·58	·03*
[16]Scarborough, tumuli and cists . . . . . SS	9·36	·01	2	4·68	·005
[6]Old Keig, Scotland . . S	14·08	·03	3	4·69	·01
[13]Sussex, other terraces near Mt. Caburn . . . EE	941·	7·	200	4·705	·035*
[7]Stones of Veu, Scotland S	9·54	·04	2	4·77	·02

Their mean is 4·70 ± ·01, and it should evidently be ×2 = 9·40 ± ·02.

(140) The following seem to be connected:—

		±			±
[1]Dorset, Winterbourne circle SS	323·	6·	100	3·23	·06*
[1]Dorset, Gorwell circle . . SS	980·	20·	300	3·27	·07*
[22]Brogar circle, Scotland EE and SS	9·87	·02	3	3·29	·007
[6]Sussex, Highdown, square pit E	9·87?	·05	3	3·29	·02
[8]Sussex, Highdown, camp divisions . . . . EE	823·	3·	250	3·292	·012*

The mean of these is 3·290 ± ·005. The last two items are from the same camp; they were entirely separately deduced, the one from dimensions of a stepped and rectangular pit in the camp, given by Col. Lane Fox, the other from the internal divisions of the camp, from my own survey. The resemblance of the units that they give is striking.

(141) The next three perhaps indicate a unit:—

			$\overset{+}{\cdot 05}$			$\overset{+}{\cdot 05}$
[8]Dartmoor, huts, &c. . . SS	15·92	·05	1	15·92	·05
[5]Yorkshire, British chariot	1·60	·01	$\frac{1}{10}$	16·0	·1
[2]Cornwall, Llanteglos, inscribed stone . . . S	16·1	·1	1	16·1	·1

Their mean is 15·95 ± ·02.

(142) In the following remains a foot appears to have been used exactly equal to the Roman 11·64 :—

		$\overset{+}{\cdot 3}$			$\overset{+}{\cdot 03}$*
[7]Stonehenge . . . SS and EE	115·4	·3	10	11·54	·03*
[6]Dorset, Cattistock, inclosures EE	1164·	18·	100	11·64	·18*
[6]Sussex, pit N.E. of Mt. Caburn . . . . E	235·	3·	20	11·75	·15*
[5]Surrey, Farley Heath Camp EE	2945·	30·	250	11·78	·12*
[2]Dorset, Chilcombe barrow . . E	238·	1·	20	11·9	·05*

The mean is 11·66 ± ·06. It can hardly be doubted that this unit is the Roman foot, by the exact similarity of its length; and it is important if this is clearly proved to be the unit of Stonehenge, as it would thus almost determine that structure to be of the date that Fergusson has with much reason assigned to it; unless this unit was introduced from the earlier Pelasgic architects who used it. The internal diameter of the Stonehenge circle is unquestionably the measured line, by the *inner* faces of the stones agreeing best to a true circle; and this diameter is exactly 100 Roman feet, being 1163 inches. The other diameters are also in very simple numbers, being just 80, 50, and 40 of these feet; the earth circles, &c., also agree to this basis. Accurate dimensions have alone been used in this inquiry, according to a detailed survey made on purpose for this object, giving the exact shape and position of every stone correct to a fraction of an inch. Stukeley's 20·8 cubit fails hopelessly when tested with accuracy; but this failure of a theory founded on inaccurate and insufficient data, should not make us distrust a result, based on evident and clear relations of the dimensions when now accurately ascertained.

(143) In the Runic stones of Denmark and Gotland some lengths recur in such a way as to suggest a metric unit; from the mean of a dozen of the best it is probably 12·80 ± ·04 inches. Now we have seen that 21·38 was decimally divided, and 12·80 is = 6 × 2·133 ± ·007; this is just a tenth of the 21·38 ± ·03, far within the limit of probable errors. Thus 12·80 is the foot of the 21·4 cubit; just as the 12·4 or Babylonian foot (so often found in classical remains) is the foot or $\frac{6}{10}$ths of the Egypto-Babylonian 20·6 cubit.

RESULTS.

(144) Thus, so far as results can be obtained from these remains, the following are the units, and the number of instances of each:—

		+		Mean
7 of	21·32	·05	France	25 of
15 of	21·48	·06	England	21·38
3 of	21·34	·04	Scotland	± ·03

$$+$$

3 of 22·56	·04	France	⎫ 20 of
11 of 22·42	·05	England	⎬ 22·51
6 of 22·53	·03	Scotland, &c.	⎭ ± ·02

4 of 20·41	·01	S.W. England.
5 of 4·70	·01	× 2 = 9·40 ± ·02.
5 of 3·29	·005	
3 of 15·95	·02	
5 of 11·66	·06	
12·80	·04	Runic. Denmark, &c. $\frac{6}{10}$ths of
		21·33 ± ·07.

The 21·3 unit seems to be the principal one in France, and the 22·5 the principal one in Scotland. There does not seem to be any difference in the character of the remains in the two groups. The "Hants, Abshot" 22·2 inch unit in England, is a block of ordinary Sarsen stone, buried under four or five feet of undisturbed stratified gravel. It is apparently wrought, having a flat face, and a tolerably rectangular side and end; the cleavage joints are not parallel to the face or side, but at an oblique angle to both; thus the surfaces cannot be those of mere natural cleavage. The length is not yet ascertained, as one end of the block is still buried in the gravel. The block in its present form has probably been first exposed to the atmosphere, then sunk below water, and finally covered with gravel; for in a crevice was found brown mould as if from decayed moss, over that white sea sand, and over all the yellow gravel. If this block be really metrical, it shows that the 22·5 unit was used before the surface gravels near the Southampton water were deposited.

The latest examples of this unit that can be dated are apparently the Brough of Clickimin, Lerwick, and Maeshowe.

It is remarkable, and I must say rather unaccountable, that the same unit should be found from North

Scotland to South England in so many cases. Perhaps more than one of these units may be merely the result of casual coincidences; but still in the two large groups there seems to be a persistent repetition of the same quantities in so many instances, that it would be hard to suppose that mere accident can have occasioned such a grouping.

(145) The units mentioned include all those yet found, except half a dozen which do not seem to belong to any group; of these, however, one is worth notice. In a bronze age tumulus at Ribe in Jutland, the coffin found, and also such of the objects in it as could be supposed to be metrical, give by inductive examination a unit of 2·92 ± ·02 inches. This is apparently a palm, of which the digit would be ·730 ± ·005 ; which is just the usual digit of the Mediterranean countries. The unit might be ¼ of the Roman foot, and thus due to Roman civilisation, 4 × 2·92 being 11·68 ± ·08.

(146) In the African remains a cromlech at Sigus was quoted, which gives 66·7 ± ·2 as a unit. It may be noticed that this is 3 × 22·23 ± ·07, which is within the 22·5 group of units. In absence of any other evidence this is not worth much; and it is better to place the Sigus cromlech along with other African remains; but still it suggests a connection which would be worth farther search.

From some megalithic remains in Sinai a unit may perhaps be deduced; the mean from 6 measures is 15·58 ± ·07.

(147) From the Ogham stones of Roovesmore 4·94 ± ·02 was deduced by 7 measures; and from the Fardell Ogham stone 8·40 ± ·07 may be deduced from its 3 dimensions.

AMERICA.

(148) The North American earthworks are so far similar to the English, that the preceding observations apply to them in a great degree.

We will first notice some of the geometrical relations of these works. Squier, in his researches on these remains, has noted that there are five or six instances of squares which are of an equal size, though at considerable distances from each other; on looking over the measures that he gives I find no less than eleven instances of the same length, 1,050 or 1,080 feet.

Not only is there this resemblance in linear dimensions, but, as Squier has pointed out, the areas of the figures are in some cases equal. At Hopeton, for instance, there is a rectangular inclosure which is equal in area to a circular inclosure connected with it; this is correct within ᵗ₅₀th, which is much less than the uncertainty of the measures. There are in all six circles of this same size.

A peculiarity of the Hopeton earthworks is that one side of the rectangle intersects the circle; Squier describes this, but has not noted the following simple relations:—The length of the chord thus produced (A B) is closely equal to the radius of the circle, A B being 530 feet, against A C 525 feet ($\frac{1}{2}$ of 1,050 feet); thus A B C is an equilateral triangle. Farther, the length of the

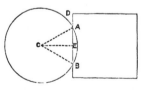

side of the rectangle is just double the distance from the centre of the circle to the side of the rectangle, C E being 455 feet, and D E 450 feet. The errors of the measurements probably quite cover these 5 foot differences. As this length of the side of the rectangle thus geometrically fixed would not give a true square equal in area to the circle, the other dimension of the rectangle is longer, 950 feet instead of 900; so that thus the areas are exactly equal.

This is not merely one chance coincidence out of a large amount of material for examination; but is the relationship existing in a unique case of juxtaposition of earthworks. There seem to be many other connections between the areas of the North American earthworks; but the measurements as yet made are so far rough, that for *areas* not very much can be safely deduced from them.

(149) Having thus pointed out some of the geometrical relations which exist between these remains, we will proceed to notice how far they agree to a metric unit (see Introduction). On carefully examining them it seems that the continually-recurring length of 1,050 or 1,080 feet is 1,000 units. The multiples which appear to have been used are of a very simple character, being principally round hundreds, and sometimes quarter hundreds. On separately examining some of the very best measures, which are *stated* to within about a hundredth of their whole lengths, the unit deduced from them varied from 12·50 to 12·72 inches, with a mean of 12·60 ± ·02: this is a small extent of variation considering the likely errors of measurement; it is, in fact, an *extreme* difference of *less* than 1 per cent. of the whole amount on each side of the mean, in measures which, on their best showing, are, on an *average*, only correct to about 1 per cent.

To this unit all the remains described by Squier agree, as closely as the nature of the measures would lead us to expect; some 70 or more of the best measures having been compared.

(150) On looking at the best measurements of small articles of the mound-builders, we may, perhaps, descry this same unit. I only refer here to measures of more accuracy than $\frac{1}{70}$th of their whole length. Some of the best measured articles are plates of copper $7\frac{1}{2}$ and $8\frac{1}{2}$ by $4\frac{1}{4}$ inches; here the $4\frac{1}{4}$ and $8\frac{1}{2}$ are clearly as $1:2$, and farther $4\frac{1}{4} + 8\frac{1}{2} = 12\frac{3}{4}$, closely the same as the unit of $12\cdot60$, which is thus divided by 3. In fact, applying this unit to *all* the more accurate measures given by Squier, we find a near connection:—

		As measured.	By unit.	
Copper plates	$\{$	$8\frac{1}{2}$	$8\cdot4 = \frac{2}{3}$ of $12\cdot60$.	
	$\times\ 4\frac{1}{4}$	$4\cdot2$	$\frac{1}{3}$	,,
		$7\frac{1}{2}$	$7\cdot4$	$\frac{7}{12}$,,
Adzes	$\{$	$6\frac{1}{3}$	$6\cdot3$	$\frac{1}{2}$,,
	$\times\ 2\frac{1}{3}$	$2\cdot1$	$\frac{1}{6}$,,
Stone tube . . . long		$13\cdot$	$12\cdot6$	1
	diam.	$1\cdot1$	$1\cdot05$	$\frac{1}{12}$
Another . . . . long		$6\cdot$	$6\cdot3$	$\frac{1}{2}$

These measures are (in all but one case) as close to the fractions of the $12\cdot6$ unit as the terms in which they are described can state them; all the fractions belong to a duodecimal method of division; and this regularity, and the close agreement of the measures, indicate a strong probability of the correctness of the unit, and of these fractional divisions.

Thus, so far as our information at present extends, there seems a considerable probability that there was anciently a unit in general use over the Northern part of the United States of $12\cdot60 \pm \cdot02$ inches, and that this was divided duodecimally.

Mexico, &c.

(151) From the few accurate Mexican measurements that I have examined it would seem that a unit of

$10 \cdot 65 \pm \cdot 04$ inches was used; this is the mean from about a dozen measures.

(152) The measures of Copan, in Central America, from the architectural remains, give a unit of $6 \cdot 817 \pm \cdot 01$. From the measures of the idols which were examined separately, and also purely inductively, a unit of $6 \cdot 713 \pm \cdot 015$ was obtained. For a mean from 16 measurements we may take $6 \cdot 76 \pm \cdot 03$.

POLYNESIA.

(153) From Ellis's measures of some of the ancient Hawaiian buildings, it would seem that they were built by measure. The few accurate measures that he gives all yield very closely the same unit; the mean by the four best is $537 \cdot 1 \pm \cdot 5$ inches. Of course this is a multiple of the unit actually handled by the builders; and judging by some of the shorter, though rougher, measures, this was probably $\div 12$; thus giving a unit of $44 \cdot 76 \pm \cdot 04$ inches.

Totally independently of this result, I had before concluded that there seemed to be a unit in the dimensions of a mound in Tahiti; and when examining the Polynesian measures I had quite forgotten it, so it could have no influence on the conclusion formed from them. The three dimensions of this mound at Oberea, Tahiti, clearly show a unit of $531 \cdot \pm 2 \cdot$ inches; the resemblance of this to the Hawaiian $537 \cdot$ unit is striking, and they confirm each other to some degree. Perhaps $535 \cdot \pm 2 \cdot$ might be fairly adopted to represent these two units; this $\div 12 = 44 \cdot 6 \pm \cdot 2$.

INDIA.

(154) The results here given, mainly from the rock-cut temples of Elora, are but a very small item

towards Indian metrology. Considering the relation of the Hindûs with the Western nations, a careful examination of the earliest Indian remains might be expected to throw as much light on Western metrology, as Indian languages have thrown on Western philology.

The following is the main group of Elora units :—

		$\pm$			$\pm$
[4]Parasu Rama	8·83	·01	5	1·766	·002
[26]Keylas	10·61	·01	6	1·768	·002
[10]Teen Tal	7·075	·006	4	1·769	·0015
[4]Do Tal	5·320	·005	3	1·773	·002
[5]Das Avatar	178·78	·08	100	1·788	·001
[6]Januwassee . . .	53·85	·05	30	1·795	·002
[7]Jugnat	5·445	·013	3	1·815	·004

The mean is 1·782 ± 004, and is apparently decimally multiplied.

(155) The only other group from Elora is—

		$\pm$			$\pm$
[7]Visvacarma	12·27	·025	15	·8180	·0015
[4]Ramawarra	4·988	·007	6	·8313	·0012
[9]Indra	33·38	·04	40	·8345	·0010
[8]Dhurma	33·86	·02	40	·8465	·0005

The mean is ·833 ± ·001, probably decimally multiplied. This group is less compact than the preceding; and perhaps the first example, 12·27, may be an accidental variation.

(156) One unit at Elora does not agree to either of the preceding groups; it is—

[3]Nilacantha . . . . 6·930 ± ·005

(157) From the best measures of the rude stone remains in the Dekhan the following units seem apparent :—

		$\pm$	$\frac{1}{10}$		$\pm$
[4]Huggeritgi.	1·833	·01		18·33	·10
[7]Rajunkolloor	18·45	·10	1	18·45	·10

These were obtained quite independently of each other, and they seem to agree; the mean is $18·38 \pm ·06$, and this is apparently the *hasta*. The fact of similar Indian and English remains both being usually in terms of 6, 12, 18, &c., feet (as noticed by Colonel Meadows Taylor in his most useful papers on these monuments), does not necessitate their having been constructed with the same unit; and it so happens that the circles of 6, 12, 18, and 36, feet are 4, 8, 12, and 24 *hasta ;* and also 18 feet is 10, and 36 feet 20, of the commonest pre-historic British unit (see 136), and the 6 and 12 feet are $\frac{1}{3}$ and $\frac{2}{3}$ of this quantity. Thus this resemblance need not lead us astray, as it is shown to be accidental by inductive examination of the kindred remains independently of each other.

(158) The ancient Indian units yet found are, therefore, as follows:—

$$\begin{array}{llll}
& & \pm & & \pm \\
7 \text{ of } & 1·782 & ·004 & \times 10 = 17·82 & ·04 \\
4 \text{ of } & ·833 & ·001 & \times 10 = 8·33 & ·01 \\
1 \text{ of } & 6·930 & ·005 & \\
2 \text{ of } & 18·38 & ·06 & \text{Rude stone in Dekhan.}
\end{array}$$

Elora.

(159) The $17·82$ unit is perhaps a variety of the *hasta* or *hath*, which is now reckoned at 18 and 19 inches. If this is so, the digit, $\frac{1}{24}$th, is $·7425 \pm ·0018$ inches. The best examples of the modern *hasta*, however, give a mean of $19·25 \pm ·04$.

The $8·33$ unit may be the half of the *aratni* mentioned in the *Markandeya Purana ;* it is there stated as 21 middle breadths of the thumb, of which 10 equalled the forefinger span, according to which data it would be about 16·8 inches, perhaps ± ·5; the double of the 8·33 unit is 16·66 ± ·02.

It may be just mentioned that the 6·930 is a quarter of a gaz of frequent occurrence in modern India, the mean value of which is 27·6 ± ·1; this is 4 × 6·90 ± ·03.

The 18·38 unit seems clearly to be a form of the *hasta;* the decimal division of it is curious and suggestive.

(160) From a carved wooden lintel of "an ancient palace," at Hangurakette in Ceylon (now in the South Kensington Museum), it appears that a unit was there used of 6·116 ± ·005. This unit agrees well to a few other Cinghalese measures, which are too uncertain to be inductively treated.

(161) Though I have no monumental evidence to produce on the subject of the Ilahi gaz, yet there are data in connection with this much-disputed unit that have not yet been brought forward.

Among other units that Abul Fazl mentions with the Ilahi gaz (defining them all apparently by the same digit), he gives the Kasbah gaz of Ibn Abililah as 24 digits, and the Yusufi cubit of Baghdad as 25 digits; whilst the Ilahi gaz is 41 digits. Now Kalkaschendi mentions the Yusufi cubit used in the buildings of Baghdad, and also the cubit of Ebn Abi Léili—*i.e.,* two that Abul Fazl mentions: and they bear the same ratio to each other in both authors, though Kalcaschendi's standard digit was rather shorter; · so that the cubits are respectively stated by him as 25⅓ and 26⅓, instead of 24 and 25, digits. The actual value given for these cubits by Quiepo (who closely agrees with Boeckh) is—

	Inches.	Abul Fazl's digits.	∴ 1 digit of Fazl. Inches.
Gaz of Ibn Abílílah . .	19·97	= 24 ×	·8320
Yusufi cubit of Baghdad .	20·78	= 25 ×	·8312
Therefore the Ilahi gaz (by mean value of digit) .	34·09	= 41 ×	8316 mean.

This derivation of the value of the Ilahi gaz seems unexceptionable, and it is pretty close to the varied modern statements of the length given in Prinsep's Tables (1858, p. 122). The value given in Marsden's Numismata Orientalia (1874) by Mr. Thomas is only based on the diameters of hand-made coins; and is, therefore, an approximation evidently of little real accuracy, as I believe that gentleman so considers it; moreover, it gives for the Ilahi gaz a length 1½ inches shorter than any found by actual measures.

(162) If, therefore, we accept this length of the Ilahi gaz from the double authority of these two cubits mentioned with it, we have for the other measures stated by Abul Fazl the following values:—

	Digits.	Inches.
Short gaz	18 =	14·9
Long gaz	24	19·9
Gaz saudá, of Harún al Rashíd	24⅔	20·5
Yusufi gaz of Baghdad	25	20·8
Ancient gaz	26	21·6
Another gaz	27	22·5
Geodetic gaz, gaz masáhat	28	23·3
Hashamah gaz (small) of Abú Músa Ashari	28⅓	23·5
Hashamah gaz (long) of Mansúr 'Abbás .	29⅔	24·6
Umríah gaz of Khalif Umr	31	25·8
Mámúnieh gaz, Mámún 'Abbásí (half) .	34¾	28·9
Ilahi gaz	41	34·1
Humáyúni gaz	41½	34·5
Another gaz	42	34·9
Akhbari gaz for cloth	46	38·3

In the absence of other accurate proof as to the original length of the Ilahi gaz, these may be adopted

K

as the best results. There is no reason to conclude that this Mohammedan digit used by Abul Fazl is the same as the digit of the original Aryan Hindûs, connected with their *hasta*.

TURKEY AND PERSIA.

(163) From some of the buildings of the Mohammedan era in these countries the units have been obtained ; the most usual unit is the following:—

	Unit.	±		Mean unit.	±
[4]Konieh, Medressé bleu . . .	17·16	·03	1½	11·44	·02
[3]Kaisarieh, mosque of Hossen .	13·85	·01	⁶⁄₅	11·54	·01
[13]Erzeroum, Imaret of Oulou Djami	11·55	·03	1	11·55	·03
[10]Broussa, mosque of Mourad I.	3·867	·004	⅓	11·600	·013
[8]Broussa, school of Mourad I.	11·67	·02	1	11·67	·02
[9]Broussa, mosque of Mourad I.	11·71	·015	1	11·71	·015
[12]Broussa, mosque of Mourad I.	11·715	·01	1	11·715	·01

The mean of these is 11·63 ± ·02. There can hardly be any doubt that this is the Roman foot, which varied from 11·64 in Asia Minor to 11·74 in Africa; the pure Roman standard was 11·64 ± ·01.

(164) The only other Asia Minor unit is

[20]Isnik, green mosque . . . 3·014 ± ·002

(165) In Persia the principal group is

		±			±
[11]Ispahan, Medressé of Shah Sultan Hussein	10·145	·01	10	1·0145	·001
[11]Tabriz, mosque of the Sunni .	5·082	·008	5	1·0164	·0016
[9]Persian house	4·088	·0055	4	1·022	·0014
[10]Deibid, Khan	5·15	·05	5	1·030	·01

Mean 1·016 ± ·001; 5·15 might seem to be too far from the group; but it has such a large probable error that there is no difficulty in thus classing it. This mean unit 1·016 is strikingly close to the ancient Persian 1·013 ± ·001, which was the most usual unit, $\frac{1}{25}$th of the Royal cubit.

(166) The following two seem connected :—

		$\pm$			$\pm$
[8]Tchimley, Karavanserai . .	12·40	·02	1	12·40	·02
[7]Sultanieh, tomb of Shah Khoda Benda	18·66	·04	1½	12·44	·03

Mean 12·41 ± ·01. A unit resembling this (12·40 ± ·01) is often found in Ancient Greece, and is the Babylonian foot; it was derived from the 20·6 cubit, which was used in Persia, and therefore it is not surprising to find this derivative of it.

(167) There are only two ·other units to be mentioned,

[8]Tchelesieh Karavanserai . . 16·889 ± ·007,

which may be compared with the ancient Persian 16·88 ± ·03;

and (168) [33]Ispahan, mosque of Mesjid Shah 13·676 ± ·014,

which may possibly be ⅔rds of a cubit of 20·51 ± ·02, a form of the old 20·6 cubit which was divided duodecimally in Ancient Persia.

RESULTS.

(169) The following, then, are the Turkish and Persian units :—

		$\pm$		
7 of	11·63	·02	Asia Minor.	11·64 ± ·01 Roman foot.
1 of	3·014	·002	Asia Minor.	
4 of	1·016	·001	Persia.	1·013 ± ·001 Ancient Persia, $\frac{1}{25}$th Royal cubit.
2 of	12·41	·01	Persia.	⅗ of 20·68 ± ·02. 20·70 ± ·04 Ancient Persia.
1 of	16·889	·007	Persia.	16·88 ± ·03 Ancient Persia.
1 of	13·676	·014	Persia.	⅔ of 20·51 ± ·02 ?

Thus it seems plain that the units used for the Mohammedan buildings of Turkey and Persia, are the ancient units used by the old Greeks and Persians in the same places. This is a suggestive fact, and points to the conclusion that the skill and habits of the artificers were *native,* and not due to the conquering Saracenic or Tatar races ; though the new masters might cause their ideas of art to be carried into effect.

CHAPTER X.

SYNOPSIS OF THE INDUCTIVE EXAMINATION.

THE HISTORY OF METRICAL UNITS.

(170) HAVING now noticed the results which have been obtained by inductive examination of the monuments of each country, it will be well to briefly gather together all those units which seem to be connected with each other, and so to form a sort of history of each unit of measure that has been used, to point out its variations, and its probable original length. The exact details of length are given in the accompanying table of results (181).

The 25-inch cubit is found in ancient Egypt, Assyria, Persia, Syria, and probably in Greece, varying from 25·1 to 25·4. In modern Persia, Arabia, Greece, Candia, Algiers, and Italy, a pic or braccio of the same length is also found, varying from 25·0 to 25·3. The possibility of this widespread unit having some connection with the Chinese foot (the double of which is 25·18 ± ·04) and with the North American mound builders' foot (½ of 25·20 ± ·04) should not be disregarded; though farther evidence, beyond these very close resemblances, is needed to prove a connection. Don Quiepo also connects with it the Japanese *inc* 75·21—*i.e.*, 3 × 25·07.

This unit was divided by 25 or 50 in Egypt and Persia, and also decimally in Greece; in fact, it seems very probable that the 25th (the *inch*, if I may so call it) was the real basis of the cubit; as there is an 8-inch mark on the Egyptian cubit rods, agreeably to the system whereby all units were shown in a binarily multiplied form on those rods. The Egyptian form of this cubit is probably nearest to the original, as being the oldest that we have, and this gives 25·10. This is well known as the sacred Hebrew, Royal Persian, and Chaldean cubit, mentioned by Newton, Golius, Kelly, Quiepo, and Oppert.

Quiepo connects with this cubit the Arabic cubit of 18·9, which he believes to be ¾ of it. The 18·9 cubit is found, as we have seen, in Egypt on the cubit rods; also binarily divided, as a 16th, in Assyria (as we should expect, all units on the cubit rods being multiples by 8 or 16); and also of full length, or divided, in Persia, Asia Minor, Greece, Africa, and Sardinia, varying from 18·92 to 19·30, which corresponds to a cubit of 25·23 to 25·73. This extent of variation does not agree with that of the 25-inch cubit, and · the connection may perhaps be considered as probable but not certain. This is the double of the ancient Pythic foot, the Greek form being within ¹⁄₁₀th inch of the length attributed to that unit. The modern Persian unit of twice 19·13, the Arabic 18·95, and the Tripoli 19·03, are probably the recent forms of this unit. The Siamese *sok* of 18·96 inches may perhaps claim connection with these; and the itinerary measure of 8,000 *soks* is apparently the same as the *dain* of Burmah, which is divided into 1,000 *dhas* of 154, or 8 × 19·25, inches.

Another unit that may be connected with the 25-inch

cubit is the 2·111 of Egypt; this is $\frac{1}{12}$ of 25·33, and is found multiplied by 8 (16·89) on the cubit rules, and also as 16·88 in Persia. The Indian 8·33 (half of the *Aratni?*) may be the half of this, or $\frac{1}{3}$ of the cubit. The values of the 25-inch cubit corresponding to these 16·8 units are from 25·0 to 25·33, and this agrees closely with the variations of the full cubit.

The 20-inch unit is perhaps another multiple of the inch basis of the 25-inch cubit; it is found in Assyria (as Dr. Oppert also shows), Syria, Asia Minor, Italy, Sardinia, and Arabia, from 19·96 to 20·24, and often decimally divided, corresponding to a cubit of 24·95 to 25·30. As this 20-inch unit was used in Roman Britain (in the form of $\frac{1}{10}$th, or two inches), it seems probable that our English inch, which corresponds so closely to it, is derived from it, as many other Romano-British measures appear to have descended. Another English unit of about 8 inches (the same length as the mark on the Egyptian cubit rods) corresponds to it also ; and possibly the ancient British 16-inch unit may be a member of the same family. These Western forms of it vary from ·995 to 1·000 British inches for the basis.

Thus the 25-inch cubit and the units probably or possibly connected with it, are :—

Ancient.			Modern.	
I. Egypt, Assyria, Persia, Syria, Greece, America ?	25·1 to 25·4	...	25·0 to 25·3	Persia, Arabia, Greece, Candia, Algiers, Italy, China? Japan ?
	or $\frac{1}{25} = \begin{cases} 1\cdot004 \\ \text{to } 1\cdot016 \end{cases}$			

| II. Egypt, Persia, Asia Minor, Africa, Sardinia . . . | 18·92 to 19·30 | ... | 18·95 to 19·13 | Persia, Arabia, Tripoli, Siam? Birmah ? |
| Supposed by Quiepo to be $\frac{3}{4} \times$ | 25·23 to 25·73 | ... | 25·27 to 25·51 | |

III. Egypt, Persia . . . 16·89
　　India . . . . . . 16·66
　　Perhaps a foot of $\frac{2}{3}$ × $\begin{cases} 25·0 \\ \text{to} \\ 25·33 \end{cases}$

IV. Assyria, Syria, Asia⎫ 19·96
　　Minor, Italy, Sardinia,⎬ to
　　Arabia . . . . . .⎭ 20·24
　　Ancient British . . . . 15·94 ?
　　Mediæval English . . $\begin{cases} 7·96 \\ ·9998 \end{cases}$ . . . 1·000 English inch.
　　　Probably multiples $\begin{cases} 24·87 \\ \text{to} \\ 25·30 \end{cases}$
　　　of the $\frac{1}{25}$th of .

So that the base of these measures is—

		Extent of variations.	Principally.
by	I.	25·1 to 25·4 or 1·004 to 1·016	25·25 or 1·010
	II.	25·2 to 25·7	25·30 or 1·012
	III.	25·0 to 25·3	25·30 or 1·012
	IV.	·995 to 1·012	25·00 or 1·000

Perhaps, on the whole, an original basis of about 25·10 ± ·05, divided into 25ths of 1·004 each, would best agree to all of these derived units; considering that the last is a very important group, and more likely to be connected with the 25-inch cubit than either the IInd or IIIrd group, and also the oldest form of the full-length cubit is 25·10.

(171) Another grand basis of metrical units is the digit. This unit is found of closely the same length in Egypt, Assyria, Persia, Asia Minor, and Italy, varying from ·728 to ·734; the most ancient form is probably about ·729 ± ·001. This unit was, as we have seen, altered in Egypt in some instances, to have an integral relation to the 20·6 cubit, though the old length was principally used; also in Greece it was altered to have a

binary instead of duodecimal connection with the Greek foot, this change most likely occurring at about the close of the epoch of Pelasgic architecture.

That the digit is connected with the Roman foot seems certain; and the latter unit was, as we have seen, identical with the unit of the Pelasgi and of the Etrurians, from whom it is commonly supposed to have descended to the Romans. The digit, or $\frac{1}{16}$ of these variations of the Roman foot and its prototypes, varies from ·721 to ·734; so close a correspondence that a connection cannot be doubted, especially in view of the Egypto-Assyrio-Phœnician origin of early Greek and Roman civilisation. The so-called pre-historic remains which have this unit may be all post-Roman; and the examples of this unit in Syrian and Turkish remains may be likewise due to the Romans. The instances found in mediæval England suggest that this unit lingered on in the country, along with other Roman units, until mediæval times.

The Olympic foot (12·14) is usually supposed to be binarily connected with a digit far longer than any other ancient digit; it has been already pointed out that, besides such a digit being otherwise unknown, 1st, the Pelasgic or "ancient Greek" foot (equal to the Roman) agrees to the usual length of the digit; 2nd, the Egyptian cubit, from which the Olympic was derived, is exactly 25 of the usual Egyptian digits, and certainly cannot be 24 of any digit used in Egypt; there can hardly be a doubt that the digit would accompany its cubit of 25 digits in its migration to Greece; 3rd, the Olympic foot is simply connected with the old digit, 6 feet, or 4 cubits, being 100 old digits. The digit thus given by the Olympic foot varies from ·727 to ·730, in exact accordance with the known variations of the digit. The Olympic foot appears to have been carried by the Romans (perhaps Greek legionaries) into Africa and Britain, and to have descended to mediæval England. It is remarkable that the Egyptian, Greek, and Roman instances of the Olympic foot and cubit all give 12·16 and 12·17; this suggests that perhaps the Parthenon standard of 12·14, though true for Athens, may be abnormally short. The Cinghalese unit, 6·12, may just possibly be connected with the Greek conquests in India; it is more likely to be ⅓ of the *hasta*. We need more Indian evidence to show that the present *hasta* was not the Olympic cubit, introduced under the Greek dynasties.

Thus the digits and units connected with it are:—

I. Egypt, Assyria, Asia Minor, Persia, Italy . . . . . $\left.\right\}$ to $\left\{\begin{array}{l}·728\\·734\end{array}\right.$

II. Pelasgic Greece, Etruria, Rome, Mediæval England $\left.\right\}$ $\begin{array}{l}11·52\\\text{to } 11·74\end{array}\left.\right\}$ $16 \times \left\{\begin{array}{l}·721\\\text{to }·734\end{array}\right.$

III. Egypt, Greece, Italy, Mediæval England . . . . $\left.\right\}$ $\begin{array}{l}12·14\\\text{to } 12·17\end{array}\left.\right\}$ $\tfrac{100}{8} \times \left\{\begin{array}{l}·728\\\text{to }·730\end{array}\right.$

Probably the original digit may be best represented by ·729 ± ·001, considering its various forms. The close agreement of its length in different countries and nations, clearly proves that a definite standard was used and communicated, and that the fingers of each nation did not originate their respective digits.

(172) One of the most generally known of all ancient units is the 20·6 cubit, called the Royal Egyptian, Karnak, or Babylonian cubit. This is found in Egypt, Assyria, Persia, Syria, Asia Minor, and even in Roman Gaul. It varied from 20·60 to 20·73, and the most ancient examples, Egyptian and Assyrian, closely agree with the Egyptian mean of 20·64. This cubit was generally divided decimally in Egypt, Assyria (as in the

most ancient cylinder of Dungi), in Persia, and Asia Minor. The division into 28 digits was, as has been already shown, an arrangement for the connection of the digit, an independent unit, which was modified to fit the cubit. This altered length of the digit is perhaps also found in Sardinia, but not elsewhere.

From this cubit we find derived in Persia a unit of $\frac{1}{12}$ = 1·73, and this was multiplied by 10 in Asia Minor, forming a unit of 17·25. That this was really connected with the 20·6 cubit is evident from its being × 24, as used in Persia, and the duodecimal division may have originated in Babylonia. The corresponding values of the cubit are from 20·70 to 20·76.

Another unit derived from 20·6 is the foot of 12·40. This is known as the " Babylonian foot," and was derived from the usual decimal division of the 20·6 cubit by the common Babylonian multiple 6; it is the most usual foot in Greece, and is often found there divided by 6, = 2·06. It varies from 12·40 in Greece to 12·45 in Roman use; corresponding to a cubit of 20·67 and 20·75. It seems to have survived in England into mediæval times; and it is also found in modern Persia.

A unit of 1·547 in Egypt seems to be also derived from the 20·6 cubit; it is the $\frac{1}{8}$th of the Greek and Babylonian foot of 12·40, and remembering how the small units were binarily multiplied in Egypt, it may very possibly be the prototype of that unit.

Thus the units connected together are :—

I. Egypt, Assyria, Persia, Syria, Asia Minor . . . . . . $\Big\}$ to $\Big\{$ 20·60   to   20·73

II. Persia, Asia Minor . . . $\Big\{{}^{1\cdot725}_{\text{to }1\cdot730}\Big\} \times 12 \Big\{{}^{20\cdot70}_{\text{to }20\cdot76}$

III. Greece, Italy, Mediæval England . . . . . . $\Big\{{}^{12\cdot40}_{\text{to }12\cdot47}\Big\} \times \frac{10}{6} \Big\{{}^{20\cdot67}_{\text{to }20\cdot78}$

IV. Egypt   1·547   ×   8   =   12·38   × $\frac{10}{6}$ 20·63

The most ancient examples in Egypt and Assyria closely agree on a value of 20·63 ± ·01, and the higher values of the groups II. and III. are probably due to the increase of this unit, which took place in later times.

(173) A very widespread unit is that which Dr. Oppert has determined to be the Assyrian cubit. This is found in Egypt, Persia, Italy, and Sardinia, varying from 21·37 to 21·60. In Ireland a similar unit is found, 21·34; this is probably a descendant of the usual cubit of the pre-historic remains, which was 21·3 in France, 21·48 in England, and 21·34 in Scotland. The close agreement of these quantities with the classical unit is striking, and seems to go far to prove a connection. The Mexican half of 21·30 is also remarkably similar; and uncertain as this may be, any connection of Mexico to the Old World is valuable. The Arabic Black cubit of 21·30 is probably derived from this Oriental unit. The nearest approach to the original unit is probably 21·38 ± ·01.

(174) Another very usual unit is the 13·2, which seems to be that known as the Drusian foot. In Egypt (by induction, as well as on the cubit rods), Syria, Asia Minor, Greece, Italy, Africa, and Sardinia this is frequently found, varying from 13·19 to 13·45. The 13·22 unit, which is the most usual in mediæval England, is probably a later form of this, through the Romans; as also the Stambouli cubit appears to be, having descended in Asia Minor, and been adopted by the Turks. The original length of this unit was probably 13·22 ± ·02.

(175) The Plinian foot is found in ancient Egypt, divided by 16, and marked on the cubit rods. It is also found in Asia Minor; and the length assigned to the common Hebrew or Rabbinical cubit is the double of

this, and is also known as the Arabic cubit *belady*. This may probably be put at 10·85 ± ·02 for the original length.

(176) Another unit shown on the Egyptian cubits is the 13·89, found as ⅔ of this by the monuments; this appears to be the Philetairean foot, which has been variously stated at from 13·7 to 14·0 inches. Don Quiepo connects the Chinese covid of 14·1 or 14·4 inches with this unit; but the difference is such that in absence of farther proof we may hesitate at accepting it.

(177) An interesting unit not found in Egypt is the 11·1 foot. This is found in Syria, Punic Africa, and Sardinia; and is; from this distribution, probably of Phœnician origin. It is suggestive, therefore, to find that this is a very common unit in the pre-historic remains of France and Great Britain. The Mediterranean forms of it vary from 11·07 to 11·16, and we find it in France as the double of 11·28, in England 11·21, and Scotland 11·26; this is so near, that in the absence of any direct Phœnician examples we may well suppose these to be all varieties of the same unit. It is remarkable that in Polynesia a unit of exactly four times the Punic standard should be found; is this a coincidence? or may farther researches suggest that Phœnician traders going to the Labadian or Sindæan Isles may have wandered far, or been storm-driven, into the Pacific? The original Phœnician was about 11·17 ± ·03 probably.

(178) Another unit, 17·9, seems to be purely Aryan; being restricted to Asia Minor, Greece, and probably India;·this may be the original form of the Indian *hasta*, as it is found frequently at the Elora temples. 17·88 ± ·02 appears to be nearest to the original.

(179) The 5·65 unit found in Syria, Asia Minor, and

Greece in different forms, may by a remote possibility be connected in its Greek form of 1·131, with the Central American 6·76 or 6 × 1·127.

The remaining units found seem to be restricted to one country, and therefore do not call for observation here, beyond the suggestion that the ·749 or long Egyptian digit may have been brought by Egyptian legionaries into Britain, and so originated the ·750 Romano-British digit.

It may be generally observed that of all units found in more than three classical countries 6 of the 7 are found in Egypt; and 5 of these are marked as cubits, &c., on the cubit rods. This shows the immense importance of Egyptian civilisation in its bearings on the Mediterranean nations; for either these units originated in Egypt, and were thence carried to other countries, or else they were adopted from foreigners for commercial purposes; but this latter supposition is very unlikely, as 6 of these units were in use as early as the 4th Dynasty, the time of the earliest extant remains.

(180) Finally, the probable originals of the most important and widespread units are :—

Inches.				Mètres.		
25·10	±	·05	=	·6373	±	·0013
·729	±	·001		·01851	±	·00003
20·63	±	·01		·5238	±	·0003
21·38	±	·01		·5429	±	·0003
13·22	±	·02		·3357	±	·0005
10·85	±	·02		·2755	±	·0005
11·17	±	·03		·2830	±	·0008
17·88	±	·02		·4540	±	·0005

(181) See "Table of Units found by Inductive Examination from the Monuments."

SYNOPTIC TABLE OF THE UNITS OF MEASURE FOUND BY INDUCTIVE EXAMINATION OF THE MONUMENTS. IN BRITISH INCHES.

The material originally positioned here is too large for reproduction in thi reissue. A PDF can be downloaded from the web address given on page iv of this book, by clicking on 'Resources Available'.

GENERAL RESULTS.

(182) The average error of workmanship has been obtained for but a few countries, as I have only worked it from those remains which I have measured myself. The average error in the use of each mean unit—*i.e.*, in each group of units—was first obtained; thus giving about 5 or 10 separate averages for each country, in order to see whether any one unit was specially accurately or inaccurately used. The general mean for each country is here given; the results for the average error of workmanship are in terms of

The length of the unit = 1000	
In Egypt	6
Assyria	10
Greece	4
Roman Britain	5
Mediæval England . .	8
or separately {before 1400	9
{after 1400	4
Pre-historic remains . .	10

Thus, for instance, if the four sides of a square are respectively 98, 100, 100½, and 101½ inches, the mean is 100, and the sum of the differences 4, which ÷ number of measures is 1; *i.e.*, the mean error of workmanship is 1 in 100 or $\frac{1}{100}$; and this amount of accuracy is that found on an average in the Assyrian and Pre-historic remains.

It seems, therefore, taking nations, and not individual specimens of good or bad artisans, that the Greeks worked most accurately, their mean error being only $\frac{1}{250}$, the same as the English after A.D. 1400, which date is about the turning point in English accuracy: the Romans and Egyptians come next to them; the mediæval English before 1400, next; and the worst of all are the

Assyrians, and equal to them, the pre-historic earth-workers and stone-hewers of England, whose average error was $\frac{1}{100}$th. The pre-historic mean is that from the two largest groups, the others not being considered sufficiently certain to be fairly included. It is astonishing to find that the average error made in laying out the earthworks by the ancient British was not more than that made by the civilised sculpturing Assyrians; and it must raise our opinion of their capabilities to find that in earthworks, &c., they only made three times the average error of the most accurate nation, the Greeks. The irregularity of Assyrian work, its frequent skewness, bulging lines, and want of symmetry, are evident on the first glance; and the plans of many British earthworks, the cutting of the blocks of Stonehenge, and other monuments, will quite bear comparison with many of the Assyrian remains.

(183) It will be well to point out, finally, what has been attempted or achieved in this essay, and what are the most promising lines for farther research.

1st. The theory of probabilities has been practically applied to metrology, thus enabling true definiteness and precision to be substituted for frequent haziness and uncertainty. Diagrams of the data and their probable errors, from which results have to be drawn, are also introduced here as a means of research.

2nd. The methods of inductive examination from the monuments have also been explained in detail, and applied practically, so as to ascertain their correctness and value.

3rd. By these means the exact values of the Sacred

Hebrew or Royal Persian cubit, the Royal Egyptian cubit, the Egyptian digit, the Assyrian "hu" or " U," the ancient Greek foot, the Olympic foot, the Drusian foot, the Plinian foot, and the Pythic foot, have been ascertained from the monuments, along with the probable errors of these determinations.

4th. The following measures have been found in more extended use than was previously known. The Sacred Hebrew or Royal Persian cubit is found to have been used in Greece, Mohammedan Persia, and apparently by North American mound-builders.

The Pythic foot is found to be an Egyptian measure used also in Assyria, Persia, Asia Minor, Africa, and Sardinia. Its Arabian form is connected by Quiepo with the Hebraio-Persian cubit.

The Assyrian "great U" of Oppert is found in Syria, Asia Minor, Sardinia, and Roman Britain, and is very probably the basis of mediæval English units, including the British inch.

The digit has been found in Assyria, Persia, and Syria, and shown to be independent of the Royal Egyptian cubit.

The Roman foot has been found in Syria, Asia Minor, and Greece; and its identity with the Pelasgic foot (as well as the Etruscan cubit) exhibited.

The Olympic foot has been found in Asia Minor and Roman countries, as well as in mediæval England, and its origin from the ancient digit pointed out.

The Royal Egyptian cubit is found to have been used in Assyria, Persia, Syria, Asia Minor (agreeing with what Herodotus states), and Roman Gaul.

The Babylonian foot, derived from the regular decimal division of the Egypto-Babylonian cubit, is found to have been the principal unit in Greece, to have been used by the Romans, and to have been continued in England, principally as a Saxon unit; it was also used in Mohammedan Persia.

The Assyrian cubit (as determined by Oppert) is found to be an ancient Egyptian unit, used also in Persia, Italy, and Sardinia; and it is also identical with the early Christian Irish unit, the commonest unit of pre-historic remains, and the unit of Mexico.

The Drusian foot is found to be also an Egyptian unit, and to have existed in Syria, Asia Minor, Greece, Italy, Africa, and Sardinia, and to be apparently the origin of the most usual measure in mediæval England.

The Plinian foot is found to be of Egyptian origin, and to have been used in Asia Minor.

The Philetairean foot is likewise found first in Egypt.

The ancient Indian hasta has probably been determined, and is found to be an Aryan unit also used in Asia Minor and Greece.

5th. Many other units, the knowledge of which had dropped out of the ancient literature on the subject, have been again brought to light.

1·730, the duodecimal division of the Royal Egyptian cubit, is found as a unit in Persia and Asia Minor.

16·88, an Egyptian and Persian unit, is, probably, the ⅖, or foot, of the Royal Persian cubit. It is, perhaps, also the Indian *aratni*.

5·65 is a unit of Syria, Asia Minor, and Greece, apparently unconnected with any other unit.

11·17 is a Phœnician unit, used in Syria, Africa, Sardinia, and pre-historic remains; also identical with the ancient Polynesian unit.

·750 is an Egyptian form of the digit, also used in Roman Britain.

About a dozen other units have also been found, but each restricted to one country.

These, then, are some of the lost elements of metrology, which literature could never have restored.

6th. The probability of connections between units of various countries has been considerably removed from the region of mere conjecture towards that of circumstantial proof, by ascertaining the exact values of units in each country, and the probability of any given variation occurring. The various connections of units mentioned above do not exceed the variations which exist in the recognised use of those units.

7th. By inductive examination the units of many remains and nations, of whose origin and connections we are ignorant, have been recovered; and the methods shown to be capable of wide application, thus furnishing a new instrument of historical and ethnographical research.

8th. The average error of workmanship among different nations has been partly shown; and it gives a new standard of civilisation.

9th. All the marks on the Egyptian cubit rods have been proved to mark cubits and units, which are recovered by inductive examination from the monuments, and which are probably the prototypes of the greater part of the units used by the ancient Mediterranean nations.

Among the results of inductive examination which are suggestive of historical connections, may be instanced the exact identity of the American mound-builders' unit with the Hebraio-Persian cubit, which had a wide and ancient diffusion in the Old World. The close similarity of the Mexican unit, with the widespread 21·4 unit of the Old World; and the similarity also of the pre-historic British, and the Christian Irish unit to this. The close similarity of the Phœnician unit to a principal unit of pre-historic British remains, and also to the Polynesian unit. The identity of the Pelasgic with the Etrurio-Roman foot. The continuance of the Romano-British units into mediæval times, the resemblances being generally exact, and far within the probable errors. Also the similar continuance of the classical units into the Mohammedan times in Turkey and Persia.

Few of these results could ever have been expected from literary information apart from the monuments; and they are all suggestive of important facts in parts of history but little known at present.

All of the units stated in this essay have been *independently* found in every instance, and have not been obtained by trying whether the measures would fit to any unit known in neighbouring countries, or from other sources. The close resemblance of the quantities found in different countries may, I am aware, lead to a strong suspicion that the results were *cooked*. But I can truly state that each of the units which are grouped as all belonging together, was purely independently ascertained; and each of the groups was arranged, and its mean result determined, totally apart from any influence of the other results. The agreement of the values of the same unit in different countries is far closer than I had expected; and, in fact, I had not supposed that any unit would have been found so widely spread as many have been found to be in the course of this examination.

In almost all cases the *mean unit* is as good an exponent of the actual measures of the buildings as the simple multiples or fractions of it, which were directly obtained by induction from those measures; and accordingly it might have been substituted in all, or nearly all, cases for the units first deduced; but I preferred to give exactly the units as found before I had formed any grouping of them—and also the mean unit as determined in each country, before any comparison was made between the countries—in order to present the results without any alteration or modification, so that their agreement might serve as a simple and manifest test of their truth, and of the correctness and power of the methods of inductive examination explained in the earlier part of this essay.

These results have not been obtained from a hasty or slight examination. More than 600 buildings and other remains have been considered, and their constructors' units obtained from the mean results of over 4,000 measurements. Probably over 10,000 measurements in all have been examined, and a considerable number of them were taken by the writer, with all the accuracy requisite, for the express purpose of searching for the ancient units of measure.

Both in the taking of measurements and in the whole of these researches no bias has been wittingly allowed; the utmost endeavour has been made to avoid partiality, and the results arrived at are only those to which the materials and the methods of research naturally and clearly lead.

Farther Researches Suggested.

(184) At present but a mere sample has been taken from different countries, in order to obtain outlines for future confirmation and filling in.

The most promising lines for important results are, early India for the Aryan units; China, Cambodia, Arabia, Sardinia, Central and South America, and Polynesia, for suggestions as to the origin and connections of lost and decaying civilisations; and continental remains of the Middle Ages for the origin of modern European units, as a study of the rate of change, the extent of variation, and the natural history in general of metrological standards.

Farther examinations and accurate plans of the pre-historic remains in general are urgently needed, as they are being gradually swept away by Commons Inclosure Acts and grasping farmers. One active surveyor—amateur or otherwise—might do, for the genuine and accurate knowledge of the forms and peculiarities of our early remains, far more in three years (or perhaps even *months*) than all the antiquaries of Europe have done in as many centuries; and place the knowledge of all important facts and details, in a form beyond that wrack and ruin which Government bills can only check, but not prevent.

That the above statement may not be thought over-drawn, I would mention that there is not any collection of accurate plans of pre-historic remains, even in the British Museum (excepting those which I have deposited there), and I have only heard of one set in a private library. The plans published even in antiquarian journals are often absurdly erroneous; and very few, if any, are so detailed and accurate as to render the loss of the remains a matter of no regret to science. A plan, however, with errors of not more than 1 in 500, about as accurate as can be required for antiquarian purposes, may be easily made in two or three hours; this can be done by one person without any assistant, by the method of three fixed stations, used in nautical surveying, and the plotting can be performed by calculation as in ordinary surveys. The whole of the apparatus need not exceed 4 or 5 pounds in weight, and as many as three surveys of antiquities of ordinary extent, not over $\frac{1}{4}$ or $\frac{1}{3}$ of a mile across, may be easily done in a single day.

Thus a few industrious workers might place on record the form and details of every scrap of pre-historic antiquity that exists in the country; and enable us to form well-grounded and correct opinions, concerning the remains which have been so long discussed and fought over with the pen, after they were abandoned by the sword.

BOOKS FROM WHICH MEASUREMENTS HAVE BEEN EXTRACTED.

Adams's Malta.
Archæologia (in part).
Archæological Journal (in part).
Archæology, Congress of Pre-historic, 3rd session.
Bartle's African Antiquities.
Berbrugger's Tombeau de la Chrétienne.
Blouet's Expédition de Morée.
Borlase's Cornwall.
British Archæological Association Journal (in part).
Browne's Sacred Architecture.
Cambray's Monumens Celtiques.
Chandler's Asia Minor.
Davis's Carthage.
De le Marre's Algérie.
Dennis's Etruria.
Description de l'Égypte.
Dodwell's Tour in Greece.
Dodwell's Views of Cyclopean Remains.
Fergusson's Rude Stone Monuments.
Fergusson's History of Architecture, 2nd edit.
Flandin and Botta's Nineveh.
Flandin and Coste's Persia.
Godwin's Archæologist's Handbook.
Hoare's Wiltshire.
Hoare's Ireland.
Hunter's South Yorkshire.
Knox's Yorkshire.
Layard's Nineveh.
Lubbock's Pre-historic Times.
Lyson's Woodchester Villa.
Mediterraneo Illustrato.
Mure's Tour in Greece.
Oliver's Nuragghi Sardi.
Palestine Exploration Statements.

Petrie's Irish Architecture.
Phillips's Yorkshire.
Pooley's Glostershire Crosses.
Quarterly Journal of Science, 1872.
Rawlinson's Five Monarchies.
Rowe's Perambulation of Dartmoor.
Seeley's Elora.
Smyth's (Piazzi) Life and Work.
Squier's Aboriginal Monuments of New York.
Squier's Ancient Monuments of the Mississippi.
Squier's Antiquities of New York.
Squier's Observations on the Mounds of the West.
Squier's Observations on Peru.
Stephans and Catherwood's Central America.
Stephens' Runic Monuments.
Stuart and Revett's Antiquities of Athens, 1st and 2nd edits.
Taylor (Meadows) on Cairns in Dekhan, &c., in R.I.A. Trans.
Tennent's Ceylon.
Texier's Armenia.
Texier's Asia Minor.
Texier's Byzantine Architecture.
Thomson's The Land and the Book.
Tristram's Moab.
Tyndale's Sardinia.
Vyse's Observations at the Pyramids.
Vyse's The Pyramids of Gizeh.
Warne's Ancient Dorset.
Warne's Celtic Tumuli of Dorset.
Worsaae's Primeval Antiquities.
Wright's Celt, Roman, and Saxon.

BOOKS WHICH DO NOT CONTAIN MEASUREMENTS
USEFUL FOR METROLOGY.

Blight's Churches of W. Cornwall.

Blight's Crosses of Cornwall.

Blight's Explorations at Treveneague.

Bloxam's Principles of Gothic Architecture.

Boutell's Manual of British Archæology.

Cornwall, Royal Institute of, Antiquities in Harrier.

Davis's Tunis.

Davis's Cities of Numidia.

Gell's Geography of Ithaca.

Gell's Journey in Morea.

Harvey's Mullyon.

Hoare's Elba.

Hogg's Roman Antiquities discovered by Dr. Barth.

Macpherson's Kertch.

Saulcy's Voyage autour de la Mer Morte, &c., plates.

Smith and Porcher's Cyrene.

Steuart's Lydia and Phrygia.

Surrey Archæological Collections.

Sussex Archæological Collections.

Texier's Edessa.

Waring's Stone Monuments.

Wood's Yachting Cruise in the South Seas.

M

ADDENDA.

WHILE this essay has been in the press, over a hundred more units have been extracted from various remains. The results cover much of the ground previously examined, and agree very closely with the conclusions here published. For some countries the number of fresh examples of a unit exceed those already given. In Egypt four more instances of the 13·19 unit are found, without appreciably affecting the mean value. In Syria six more of the 20·6 cubit give 20·66 ± ·02 for the mean. In Greece three more instances of the 17·88 unit make the mean about 17·90 ± ·02; and similarly in all other cases the fresh data do not alter the mean beyond the limits of probable error stated in the table.

The Indian 18·38 ± ·06, when ÷ 3, is 6·13 ± ·02, which is apparently the Cinghalese 6·116 ± ·005.

The Pre-historic 4·70 ± ·01, when × 10 ÷ 4, is 11·75 ± ·03, possibly the Roman foot.

The League is a Celtic measure, and is always stated at 1½ Roman miles by ancient writers; this is = 87,300 inches, or 4,000 × 21·82, which may belong to either of the two Pre-historic Celtic units, 21·38 or 22·51; though this is but a very rough statement, still it would be worth more accurate examination if farther data could be obtained.

www.ingramcontent.com/pod-product-compliance
Ingram Content Group UK Ltd.
Pitfield, Milton Keynes, MK11 3LW, UK
UKHW042152280225
455719UK00001B/302